How to Buy a Condominium or Townhouse

*Practical Advice
from a Real Estate Expert*

Denise L. Evans
Attorney at Law

SPHINX® PUBLISHING
AN IMPRINT OF SOURCEBOOKS, INC.®
NAPERVILLE, ILLINOIS
www.SphinxLegal.com

First Edition: 2006

Published by: **Sphinx® Publishing, An Imprint of Sourcebooks, Inc.®**

Naperville Office
P.O. Box 4410
Naperville, Illinois 60567-4410
630-961-3900
Fax: 630-961-2168
www.sourcebooks.com
www.SphinxLegal.com

This publication is designed to provide accurate and authoritative information in regard to the subject matter covered. It is sold with the understanding that the publisher is not engaged in rendering legal, accounting, or other professional service. If legal advice or other expert assistance is required, the services of a competent professional person should be sought.

From a Declaration of Principles Jointly Adopted by a Committee of the American Bar Association and a Committee of Publishers and Associations

This product is not a substitute for legal advice.

Disclaimer required by Texas statutes.

Library of Congress Cataloging-in-Publication Data
Evans, Denise L.
  How to buy a condominium or townhouse : practical advice from a real estate expert / by Denise L. Evans.
     p. cm.
  ISBN-13: 978-1-57248-556-3 (pbk. : alk. paper)
  ISBN-10: 1-57248-556-6 (pbk. : alk. paper)
  1. Condominiums--United States--Purchasing. 2. Row houses--United States--Purchasing. 3. Real property--United States--Purchasing. I. Title.

HD7287.67.U5E93 2006
643'.12--dc22
                                                                    2006001897

Printed and bound in the United States of America.
CHG — 10 9 8 7 6 5 4 3 2 1

Contents

Deciding Whether to Remodel
Recouping Your Investment and Closing Costs
Calculating Profit on the Sale of a Condo, Townhome, or Co-op
How Long Must You Own Your Condo Before You Can Make a Profit on Sale?
Investing in Rental Properties
Estate Planning Issues
Flipping
Overcoming Analysis Paralysis

Introduction

If you are thinking about buying a condo, townhome, or co-op apartment, you are not alone. Not long ago, interest seemed to be limited to huge metropolitan areas like New York City or resorts in Florida. Today, these shared living arrangements are extremely hot in many markets. Nearly everywhere is seeing steady, sustainable growth.

Unfortunately, resources to help buyers have not kept up with the dramatically increased demand. Many real estate agents, lenders, and even developers are still relatively unsophisticated about important differences between detached housing and common interest developments (CIDs, pronounced "sids")—condos, townhomes, or co-ops. To make matters worse, there is a lot of misinformation on the Internet, making it hard to do your own research.

This book gives you a good background in concepts peculiar to such ownership styles. It also integrates those concepts into more conventional advice about shopping for and financing any home. If you have prior experience buying houses, you will see that some of the advice is familiar. Other things will have quirky little twists to them, because of the legal technicalities of buying a unit in a CID. For that reason, it is best not to take anything for granted and skip some chapters just because you are an experienced home buyer. Read everything—you are guaranteed to learn something new and very useful in unexpected places.

A Warning about "Usually," "Normally," "Typically," and "Almost Always"

What is said in this book is true most of the time. That is, when talking to a national audience about a product sold in local markets—real estate—sometimes generalizations have to made. While many things about CID markets and real estate or co-op law are the same, sometimes the rules differ from one state to another. When weighing the pros and cons of the various housing or financing options evaluated, remember that I am speaking in generalities. Therefore, you must make some effort to verify that what is said in this book applies in your market as well.

Every effort has been made to ensure that all the information found in this book is current and accurate. However, tax laws, regulations, and real estate practices change over time. Therefore, before acting on any of the advice offered here, check with your real estate agent, lawyer, or accountant to make sure that "normally" applies to your situation.

Use of "Broker" and "Agent"

Although the terms *broker*, *salesperson*, and *real estate agent* are often used interchangeably, they have very different meanings. Real estate brokers are people or firms holding real estate broker licenses, which allow them to market properties for owners. In order to obtain a real estate broker's license, an individual usually must meet educational and prior work experience requirements, pass testing, and obtain certification by a state real estate board or commission. Individuals who are designated as salespersons hold salesperson licenses, which allow them to work for licensed brokers. The broker works for the consumer, and the salesperson works for the broker. A real estate agent is a broker or salesperson who represents another individual in dealings with third parties. Agents have special responsibilities of loyalty and confidentiality imposed on them by law.

In this book, the words *broker* and *agent* are used interchangeably, because it gets incredibly boring to read an entire real estate book that repeatedly says, "broker or salesperson," or that always uses the more generic "agent" when talking about these people.

Use of "Condo," "Townhome," and "Co-op"

Condominiums, townhomes, cooperative apartments, and planned unit developments are all different things. Sometimes, collectively, they are referred to as *common interest developments* (CIDs). When some piece of advice applies to all community arrangements, either "condos, townhomes, and co-ops" or "CIDs" will be used.

Use of "Your"

Common interest developments necessarily involve discussions of community property. Some property that would be considered private in detached housing situations is communal in CIDs. For example, the driveway leading to your garage is not actually yours—it is owned by everyone in the condo project. In these situations, the word *your* is used in a loose sense; it is your driveway because no one else uses it, but technically, it does not belong to you.

Mythbuster Boxes

You will find "Mythbuster" boxes throughout this book. The italicized phrase in each box is a myth that many people believe to be true about buying condos, townhomes, or co-ops. The rest of the box explains why that myth is false or only partially true, and what the real story is for each of those issues—whether it be financing, negotiating, closing, or any other part of the condo-buying process.

Share Your Experiences

If you have any questions after reading this book, or would like to share your experiences, please write to me. While every effort has been made to cover all aspects of buying your new condo, townhome, or co-op, you might have an unusual situation. Don't be bashful! I can be reached by email at **condos@bellsouth.net**.

Top 20 Questions of First-Time Condo or Townhouse Buyers

1. Is there a condo bubble, and is it about to burst?

This is the question on everyone's mind. Some markets are experiencing a feeding frenzy as speculators bid up prices in the hopes of flipping properties and getting rich. For the most part, though, the condo market is simply growing rapidly in order to catch up with traditional housing. Lifestyle changes in the American public mean people are much more willing to live in community environments. This is a trend that will be here for many, many years. Buy wisely for your own use, and do not worry about bubbles. There may be some slowdown of growth, but a catastrophic bubble burst is extremely unlikely.

2. Do I have to use a real estate agent?

You do not have to use a real estate agent. A real estate agent can help you shop more efficiently, and can aid in the negotiating process if you are uncomfortable doing that yourself. An agent can also educate you about the market in general, particular developments, school systems, and other such things. On the other hand, real estate agents will not tell you about properties for sale unless the owner is willing to pay the agent a commission (or you are willing to do this yourself). If you work with an agent, do some market research on your own in order to find such properties. Refer to Chapter 10 for more in-depth advice on this subject.

3. Can I obtain financing with a poor credit score?

Yes. "Poor credit score" is pretty relative. You might have a good credit score but just not realize it. Even people with poor credit can obtain government-assisted financing, or they can secure loans from companies that charge higher interest rates in order to compensate for the increased risk they are taking. If you do borrow from such a lender, you should plan on this being a short-term solution. Continue to work on improving your credit score, and then move that loan as soon as you are able. Refer to Chapter 7 for financing alternatives.

4. How do I find out my credit score?

Credit scores are obtained through credit reporting agencies. The three largest are Experian, Equifax, and TransUnion. By law, each is required to give you one free credit report per year. The credit report shows who your creditors are, what the high credit amount is with each one, current balances, and your history of paying them in a timely or untimely basis. You get one credit score free per year, and after that they can be obtained from the agencies for a nominal fee—usually less than $20. Refer to pages 67–71 for more in-depth advice on this subject.

5. Where is the best place to find financing?

To some extent, the answer depends on your goals and your obstacles. Mortgage brokers generally have the widest variety of options and can assist you with advice regarding alternatives. Local direct lenders, such as savings banks and credit unions, will usually have the most flexibility. Credit unions can sometimes offer below-market interest rates because they do not have to pay income taxes on the money they earn, unlike banks. Seller financing, if available, is an excellent way to obtain below-market interest rates or financing for borrowers with credit problems.

6. I am preapproved for a loan. Does that determine how much I can afford to buy?

No. It means that a particular lender has its own opinion regarding how much debt you can afford to pay each month. Your true situation may differ, depending on how motivated you are to give up other things in your life, what interest rate you are able to obtain, how much down payment you can afford, and how much your ownership costs—such as dues, maintenance, assessments, repairs and upkeep, or cooperative apartment rent—may affect your budget. Refer to Chapter 6 for a discussion of this issue.

7. What are the top three problems at condos and co-ops, and how do I protect myself?

Noise, privacy, and financial surprises are the three most common problems with condos and co-ops. Noise levels should be investigated before purchase, and can be minimized somewhat afterwards. Privacy rights will depend in part on rules governing your community, and in part on the services demanded by you. In general, the more services you expect from your community, the less privacy you will enjoy. For example, if you want cheap, high-speed Internet access through a local server, someone can monitor your surfing activities. Financial surprises come about when a community is poorly managed, does not spend enough time or money on preventive maintenance, and does not build up a reserve for anticipated expenses like roofing, parking lot resurfacing, and other such things. A prepurchase financial review and post-purchase involvement in community meetings can help prevent such surprises.

8. Will I be at the mercy of the condo association?

Just like any democracy, you are at the mercy of the majority if you are not active in government meetings, you do not stay involved, and you do not vote. To minimize the possibility of being consistently out-voted, try to buy in a community with interests similar to your own. If you are an investor looking for a rental property, buy in a place where most of the other owners are also investors. If you want to live in your unit full-time, avoid developments where most of the other owners are investors.

9. How much control will I have over my space?

The answer depends on knowing what is *your* space. In a co-op, you do not own anything at all except stock in a corporation that owns the building. With a condo, you personally own the insides of your walls, but little else. Townhome owners usually own everything, including their side of the wall between units, but might be subject to architectural review committees, which impose restrictions on exterior paint, landscaping, and so on, or homeowners associations, which decide how long the exterior Christmas decorations can stay up. To be sure about what you can or cannot do, you will have to read the Conditions, Covenants, and Restrictions for condos, the Proprietary Lease for co-ops, and the Homeowners Association Rules for townhomes.

10. Can a co-op board really kick you out if you are rude to the super?

This is an urban myth with a small amount of truth to it. Co-op boards can kick you out for something called *objectionable behavior*. Courts give the boards a great deal of latitude on this issue and defer to something called the *business judgment rule*. Generally speaking, though, it requires some sort of recurring behavior that does not improve after repeated warnings, and that affects the other tenants' peaceful enjoyment of their units or that damages the value of the property.

11. Why should I care whether there is a management company or not?

Some condo associations and co-op boards appoint members to manage finances, maintenance, enforcement, and other such issues. The argument is that they save money, because the members do not charge a fee. As a practical matter, a third-party management company that charges a fee will still save you money, because you will have professionals who can obtain the best prices for goods and services, will be able to generate accurate financial reports, and can engage in enforcement actions without worrying about offending the next-door neighbor.

12. How can I find out if a property has a history of problems?

First, ask the current owner, the governing organization, and the management company for the development or building. People might avoid mentioning things to you, but they rarely lie when asked a direct question. If you are really serious about a property, order a home inspection and a project inspection for things like elevators, the roof, the pool, and so on. Many states require sellers to provide a buyer with a property disclosure report once a contract has been signed. As a practical matter, the real estate agent usually already has a copy of the report in his or her file, and you can ask for it at an earlier stage, before you make an offer.

13. How can I be sure a new property is well built?

Ask about the length of the builder's warranties and what things will void the warranties. A longer warranty period is usually an indication the builder is comfortable with the quality of his or her work. Find out what other projects have been built by the same developer, and visit the oldest one to see what problems have appeared over the years. For your unit, invest in a carpenter's level and see if the walls are plumb (straight up and down) and the floors, countertops, and cabinets are level. If they are not, it is an indication of a sloppy attitude. Can you see the seams in the drywall? If so, that is another indication of cutting corners. Call your local inspections department to see if it has requirements for minimum thickness of concrete or asphalt in driveways. If not, ask what they recommend, and then ask more questions of the developer regarding the project. This is one big place to cut expenses to your future detriment.

14. Do I need a home inspection if I am buying a co-op apartment?

Absolutely! You might think it does not matter because the co-op board owns the entire building and is responsible for upkeep. However, your lease might make you financially responsible for repairs in your unit, even if the board retains the right to hire the contractor. In addition, a poorly maintained unit is an indication of a poorly maintained building. You are buying trouble if you purchase without knowing this and you were in a position to ask some pretty searching questions regarding the reasons for the defects.

15. How much will my monthly dues be?

There is no single answer, or even a general rule for this question. The answer could depend on the number of amenities that must be supported, as well as the philosophy regarding whether to build up reserves for future repairs or to simply worry about them in the future and pay via special assessments. Local school taxes assessed on common areas can dramatically affect annual expenses in projects across the street from each other, but in different school districts. You will have to ask this question for every home you are interested in, and also ask what is included in the annual budget.

16. Can I cancel my purchase contract if prices go down?

Yes, if you have a specific clause in your contract that says you can do so, or if you have a clause that says you can cancel if the lender's appraisal is not equal to or greater than the purchase price. Otherwise, too bad. If you do not have an escape hatch in your contract, and you then cancel your contract, you are in breach of your contract. You risk more than losing your earnest money in such a situation, because a seller could sue you for damages—the difference between your contract price and the price he or she is ultimately able to obtain, plus perhaps attorney's fees and other expenses. In some rare circumstances, the seller could obtain a court order for *specific performance* and force you to go through with the purchase.

17. Will I get the same tax deductions as traditional homeowners?

Usually you will. Even co-op owners can now obtain the home mortgage interest tax deduction for loans they obtain to buy stock in the co-op building. For more information on tax issues, refer to pages 60–64.

18. What are the most common loan-related expenses I might have?

Lenders sometimes charge something called *origination points* to cover all their out-of-pocket expenses and some additional profit. One point is equal to 1% of the loan, so an origination fee of one point on a $250,000 loan will be $2,500. Sometimes expenses will be charged separately for third-party things like appraisals, credit reports, flood zone certificates, property inspections, and title binders. In-house expenses might be things like credit review, document preparation, underwriting analysis, rate-lock fees, and other such things. All of these are negotiable. Be sure to ask each lender what expenses they charge, what expenses they collect for third parties, and what expenses must be paid in advance, even if the loan fails to close.

19. What are the most common closing expenses?

The closing agent will charge a fee for assembling all the necessary documents and conducting the closing. There will also be lender's title insurance, owner's title insurance, document preparation, wire transfer or messenger fees, transfer taxes, and document filing fees imposed by local authorities. The co-op board or condo association might impose a flip tax, and state or local government might have a mansion tax based on the sales price. Your lender will usually require tax and insurance impounds to begin building a nest egg to pay the taxes and insurance when they come due. You and your seller might have prorated expenses for things such as your share of the current month's dues that were already paid, and the seller's share of the current year's property taxes that will not be paid until well after closing. For more details, see Chapter 17.

20. Who pays the closing costs?

This depends on the wording of your contract. Everything is negotiable, depending on how motivated the buyer and the seller are. If the contract is silent, and local law does not address the issue, then the closing agent will usually allocate expenses to the party who seems most logical to bear them. For example, a transfer tax would usually be payable by the person doing the transfer—the seller. Recordation expenses would be paid by the party who cared about whether the deed was recorded—the buyer. Preparing the deed should be the seller's expense, because the seller signed a contract in which he or she promised to give you a deed. Expenses associated with a loan, such as lender's title insurance, should logically be the responsibility of the borrower (buyer). Other things, such as closing agent fees, would be shared 50/50.

Chapter 1:
The Difference Between Condos and Houses

Most people think a *condominium* is an architectural thing—an apartment unit that can be owned instead of just rented. In reality, a condo is a legal concept that defines exactly what you own by yourself and what you own in common with other people. Condos, townhomes, and cooperative apartments all have some type of shared responsibilities and expenses, and less control than the traditional single home type of ownership. However, there are small differences among them.

You will want to know the characteristics of each kind of ownership—condominium, townhome, and cooperative apartment—so you can work with real estate professionals and advise them of your likes and dislikes. Each has its own advantages, as well as its own traps for the unprepared. If you know what you are dealing with, you can ask the right questions and avoid nasty surprises.

Condominiums

Condominium ownership is an example of joint or group ownership. Every state has statutes that establish the procedures for creating a condominium and spell out the responsibilities of anyone developing a condo project. Traditional real estate law (applicable to detached housing), on the other hand, grew up over many centuries as a result of judicial decisions. Condos split up ownership into nontraditional pieces, and new laws were needed to authorize this type of real estate ownership.

In most cases, when you purchase a unit in a condo development, you get varying levels of ownership and usage rights. Usually you have:
- *exclusive ownership* of all the interior spaces of your home;
- *common ownership* of everything else;
- *exclusive usage* (but not ownership) of things like your patio and parking place;
- *limited usage* of things that sit on common land, such as HVAC units; and,
- *restricted usage* of things like plumbing and wiring.

In other words, you alone own the paint on the inside of the front wall. It can be any color that makes you happy. However, the wall itself, the front door, and the paint on the outside are owned in common with all your neighbors. You cannot demolish part of the wall to install a porch, you cannot paint the exterior some other color, and you cannot replace a picture window with casement windows that open in order to catch the ocean breezes.

These *common elements* include the structural components of the building, your front door and your windows, and the common areas (like hallways and recreational facilities). Plumbing, electrical and phone wiring, and HVAC systems are typically part of the common elements, even if all the parts are inside your four walls. All owners in the project own the common elements, together.

Example:

Sutton Place is a condo project with three buildings—A, B, and C—totaling sixty units. Buildings A and B are each multistory, but Building C has only one floor. Mr. Smith owns C–8. Because of the technicalities of condo ownership, he also owns $\frac{1}{60}$ of the elevators in Buildings A and B, and can vote on financial matters regarding the upkeep of the elevators, even though they have nothing to do with his ground-floor unit in Building C. Mr. Smith does not own any particular $\frac{1}{60}$, since no one can split the elevator into grids and point to Mr. Smith's square.

Technically, any common element can be used by any condo owner in the project, since they are all part-owners. Realistically, though, some common elements are specified as *exclusive usage* or sometimes *semi-restricted usage.* These would be things that are truly useful only to you, like your balcony, an assigned parking place, or a locker in a fitness center. It would be unfair to allow other owners the use of those areas. Other things are defined as *restricted usage*, such as plumbing and wiring. It is generally not a good idea to let owners get too involved with potentially dangerous home maintenance, so those things are restricted. All of these access rights and restrictions are spelled out in the condominium documents, and you will be able to read them before a purchase.

Your use of the common areas—which includes the air others must breathe—is governed by a set of rules. Smoking might be prohibited, even in your own unit, if the recycled air would affect other owners. Further, any activities that might impact overall property values will also be controlled.

It is helpful to think of a condo project as a small government unit, maybe as if it were a village. There are always three different levels of internal condo law. The first is the *Declaration of Condominium*, which is the most general and is sort of like the U.S. Constitution. This document lays the groundwork for condo owner- ship, and must be filed with state or local government authorities. Most states require the following items in the Declaration:

MYTHBUSTER

Condos are always apartments

Houses can be condos if the proper legal work is done at the beginning of the development. For example, it is a common practice in retire- ment communities to build garden home condos on small lots. From the outside, they look like typical subdivisions, but homeowners do not own their driveways, lawns, shrubberies, roofs, or exterior walls. In return, someone else mows the lawn weekly, cleans the gutters periodically, repaints the house every three or four years, and so on.

- ◆ a survey of the land, showing placement of the improvements;
- ◆ floorplans of the units;
- ◆ a description of the amenities (tennis courts, pools, etc.);
- ◆ a description of things that will be owned exclusively;
- ◆ a description of the common elements;

- a description of the semi-restricted elements;
- a description of easements;
- establishment of a condo owners association;
- a description of voting rights; and,
- any plans for using vacant land to build additional units in the future.

The next level of internal condo law is the *Bylaws*, which provide a lot more detail about officers, elections, votes necessary for different types of actions, and other governance issues. The third document is called the *Conditions, Covenants, and Restrictions* (CC&Rs). Here, your rights and responsibilities are spelled out in painstaking detail.

Often there is also a fourth set of rules, called *House Rules* or something similar. The rules have the hours the pool will be open, the current schedule for pest control, and other routine matters.

Every condo project has a *condominium association*. It is the governing and enforcement body of the community. All unit owners automatically become members of the condo association. The association has periodic elections for officers and committee members, who handle most of the routine work between scheduled meetings. The association does not actually own any of the common elements. It is important to remember this, because you cannot afford to let the association do whatever it wants with common areas. You will be a part-owner, and as such, you will be expected to make responsible decisions—just as you would for your own home.

Example:

A tornado destroys the clubhouse. The insurance company pays a huge claim for the destruction. The association votes to take the insurance money and not rebuild, because the clubhouse was never used. You are in favor of that, but you wonder who gets the insurance money. Does it go into the association's *slush fund* to defray future maintenance expenses and lower the monthly fees, or does every owner get his or her pro rata share of the money right away? It might make a difference if you are planning to sell your unit next month, because you do not care about future expenses— you want money now. The particular governing documents in place at the project will help determine how the insurance money is distrib-uted. The important thing is for you to remember that you are a part-owner, and therefore, may have important rights you should discuss with an attorney.

Townhomes

The *townhome*, sometimes called a *row house* or *town house,* combines features of both single family ownership and condo ownership. Like a stand-alone home, ownership of a townhome includes both the dwelling and the piece of land on which it is built. It is like a condo because there are shared elements, but unlike a condo because there is no shared own-ership. The thing that defines a townhome is a common wall that con-nects it to another townhome. Think of two traditional houses on small lots, but smashed up tightly against each other so there are no side yards—just a wall they share in common. This common wall, known as a *party wall,* runs the entire length of the adjoining homes.

Individuals own their unit, including the outside walls and roof, and the land on which the unit is built. They also own the portion of the party wall built on their land, and they have *easement rights* in the portion built on the neighbor's land. An easement is a right to use land without actually owning or renting it. As a practical matter, the party wall easement means your neighbor cannot bulldoze his or her town-home and his or her half of the party wall in order to build a slightly smaller, freestanding home. He or she owes you the obligation of sup-porting your half of the party wall.

Usually, in a row of townhomes, one roof structure will cover sev-eral units. Owners have a responsibility to maintain their own roof in such a manner that it does not cause leaks into their neighbor's home.

There may be other jointly owned common elements in a town-home development, such as sidewalks, driveways, and fences between homes. These are treated just like the party walls. Your neighbor cannot dig up his or her half of the driveway in order to plant pansies.

Sometimes townhome communities will have areas shared by every-body—much like a condo—owned by a separate *homeowners association.* In a condo project with twenty units, each person owns one-twentieth of the common areas. A townhome owner does not own any of the common areas—the homeowners association does.

You do not need any particular legal documents in a pure townhome project that has no common recreational facilities. However, if there is a homeowners association—used to maintain common areas or just to collect dues for the annual holiday parties—it must be created by a legal document, much like a corporation. Usually it comes into being with a Declaration of Homeowners Association, which is filed in the public records of the appropriate state, county, or parish. The Declaration defines the rights and responsibilities of members. The association generally has the power to collect dues and to engage in enforcement actions against delinquent members.

Major Differences Between Condos and Townhomes

A townhome owner owns his or her own building exterior. A condo owner does not own his or her building exterior—only the things *inside.* The townhome owner might not be able to paint the siding bright orange because of association rules. The condo owner cannot paint the siding bright orange because it is not his or her siding. These might seem like silly distinctions, except in two important situations.

1. A fire destroys your unit. Whether you have enough insurance depends on who is going to have to pay to rebuild the exterior walls and roof and replace all the windows and doors.
2. The association gets lazy about enforcing rules. You want to paint the siding orange. You can—if you own the siding. You cannot, if you do not own the siding. It has nothing to do with association rules any longer, but with ownership rights.

Co-op Apartments

Co-ops have been very popular in the Northeast, especially in Manhattan. They are almost always apartments; it would be very unusual to mistake a co-op for a house. You might confuse a condo and a co-op, though, until you investigated.

The thing that makes a co-op different from a condo is how it is owned. If you want a co-op unit, you must buy stock in the corporation that owns the entire building. Only then will you be allowed to rent a particular unit from the corporation. This is called a *proprietary lease.* You do not actually own anything at all in or around your apartment, except the stuff brought by the moving van or purchased afterwards.

The tenant still pays rent, but it is usually significantly less than rents in regular apartment buildings. That is because the total rental income for the building only needs to cover things like the mortgage on the building, building utilities and maintenance, reserves for repairs, and other such things. There is no building owner trying to make a profit, because all the tenants are the owners.

The building corporation has a board of directors, just like any other corporation. The board operates very much like the officers in a homeowners association or the officers in a condominium association. It also has bylaws governing the operation of the co-op, enforcing lease terms, and maintaining common areas. The board of directors is elected by the tenants-stockholders.

Co-op tenants can sell their stock, and the accompanying rights to rent a particular apartment, but only with the approval of the board of directors. Boards cannot discriminate on the basis of race, religion, gender, and so on, but they can discriminate for other reasons. They might blackball celebrities, for example, because the other owners do not want to deal with the headaches of reporters and photographers showing up at all hours of the day and night. Co-op boards can also refuse to allow a sale to someone with a criminal background or someone who does not meet their very strict financial requirements. New York co-op boards are famous for being very choosy about who they allow in as neighbors.

The ability to control and veto sales of stock was traditionally the province of only co-op apartments. Today, condo associations are starting to amend their bylaws and give themselves the same rights, arguing that historic laws against *restraints on alienation* (restrictions on sale) do not apply to them because of the passage of specialized condominium statutes that do not mention the subject. In the future, look for this difference between condos and co-ops to be less of a difference.

Selling tenants must usually share some of the sale proceeds with the building corporation, whether or not they make a profit. This is called a *flip tax* (although it is not really a tax—just a fee). This fee can be a flat rate per share, a flat fee per transaction, or a percentage of the sale price or the profit. Percentages can vary widely from one co-op to another, but typically range from 30%–70% of the sales price. The higher the percentage retained by the corporation, the lower the potential profit from a stock sale. If a sharing percentage were 50%, the seller and corporation would split the proceeds from sale equally. If the former owner paid $120,000 for the apartment, he or she would have to sell it for $240,000 just to break even. On the other hand, if a co-op building makes larger profits on the sales of stock, then it can charge cheaper rents for the individual apartments.

Once again, condo associations are learning from their co-op apartment cousins. In recent years, there has been some limited growth in the number of condo associations that charge a transfer fee upon sale of a unit. A California court, for example, held that imposition on a condo owner of a $5,000 transfer fee was a reasonable means of revenue generation. Whether or not the flip tax continues to be a difference between condos and co-ops will depend on how other courts view the practice.

One drawback to co-op ownership is the risk of foreclosure on the whole building, rather than your individual apartment. Suppose the corporation has a $20,000,000 mortgage on its building. Somebody embezzles or mismanages corporate funds and the loan goes into default. Of course, you do not have $20,000,000 to pay off the bank. The bank forecloses and you now have a lease with a corporation that does not own anything. You can strike a deal with the bank or other new owner, but they might have

MYTHBUSTER

Tax laws are not fair to co-op owners

The tax laws used to be very unkind to co-op owners, but that is no longer the case. Generally speaking, co-op owners may now deduct interest on loans used to buy their stock, just as homeowners can deduct interest on their home mortgages. They may also exclude up to $500,000 of profit (for married people, $250,000 for singles) upon a sale, the same as house and condo owners. Additionally, they may deduct their pro rata share of the mortgage interest paid by the corporation on the building loan, and their share of the real estate taxes. (IRS publication 530 explains the rules in detail.)

other plans for the building or they might want a much larger rent. You are at their mercy. It is rare, but it could happen.

On the plus side, co-op apartments are highly desirable. They are widespread in New York City and Florida, and generally enjoy the best locations in the most historic and interesting buildings. It is not very easy to sell co-op stock, so the occupants of the building tend to be long-term, rather than trading up every few years. Once a building develops a character of its own, it usually stays that way.

Major Differences Between Co-ops and Condos

In comparison with the other forms of ownership described in this book, co-op apartments are typically cheaper to buy, but the monthly rent or dues are much higher. The following example compares a condo, a co-op, a townhome, and a regular apartment of similar sizes and qualities. These numbers are made up, so do not use them as ratios for your buying decisions. This is merely an example of how the various costs compare.

Financial Comparison of Condo, Co-op, Townhome, and Apartment

	PURCHASE PRICE	RENT	DUES	REPAIRS AND MAINTENANCE
Condo	$350,000	0	$500	$100
Co-op	$250,000	$1,500	0	0
Townhome	$300,000	0	$125	$300
Apartment	0	$4,000	0	0

The other important difference between condos and co-ops has to do with the possibility of change. Because condo owners have fewer restrictions on their ability to resell, a complex can change atmosphere almost overnight. It might go from two-income childless couples who live in their units to absentee owners renting out to single-income families with young children. There is nothing undesirable about this, unless you wanted to live in a community of residents with many common interests and social interactions. Co-op boards, who must approve any new owners, can effectively put the brakes on change. This is a benefit for some people and a drawback for others.

Planned Unit Developments

A *planned unit development* is a combination of traditional home ownership with shared amenities. Typically, people own their homes and the land on which they are built. A separate association or corporation owns common areas, such as recreational facilities, private roads in gated communities, and perhaps sprinkler or waste management systems. Homeowners pay a set monthly fee to support some or all of these things, and might additionally pay usage fees for other things, such as stables, marinas, and airplane hangars.

Planned unit developments (PUDs—pronounced as a word) usually include some aspect of mixed-use. In other words, the developer probably envisioned an old-fashioned community with a great variety of ownership options, all engineered to the proper ratios and all within walking distance of each other. There will be subdivisions of varying price ranges, retail shopping, office space, and recreational facilities. Even if there is no local zoning, PUD restrictions will prevent changes to the engineered ratios—people will not be allowed to convert houses to offices, retail spaces to hotels, or restaurants to boutiques.

Buying real estate in a planned unit development is somewhat like buying a condo because of the sharing of amenities and expenses, the controls placed on individualism, the imposition of dues and assessments, and the high degree of homeowner focus on preserving property values. If you are thinking of living in such a development, most of the condo parts of this book will provide helpful guidance.

Common Interest Developments

Condos, townhomes, co-ops, and planned unit developments are sometimes called, generically, *common interest developments* (CIDs). Their common characteristics are some type of individual occupancy teamed up with shared finances, governance, and amenities.

There is a growing trend among states to replace outdated condominium laws with the more modern *Uniform Common Interest Ownership Act*. This act provides greater protections to a wider variety of ownership options than the older Uniform Condominium Laws. That is why many of the differences among condos, townhomes, and co-ops are becoming blurred. When obtaining advice, be careful, because some lawyers tend to quit learning outside their area of expertise once they graduate from law school. Someone might give you advice that used to be true in your state, but is no longer correct because of the changed laws.

If you are looking for information on the Internet, sometimes it is easier to search on the generic term *common interest development* instead of each different type of ownership. For example, the Community Associations Institute maintains a website at **www.caionline.org** (you can also call them at 888-224-4321) that has a wealth of useful information and helpful resources. If you searched for "condo information" you might never find this website, but "common interest development" will turn it up for you.

Chapter 2:
Different Types
of Condo Developments

There are many different kinds of condominiums, and they appeal to a wide variety of buyers. In effect, the condo market is really made up of many submarkets, with different personalities. The vast majority of condos are owner-occupied and used as principal residences. Increasingly, though, a growing demand for more specialized developments—including vacation and recreational condos, retirement condos, and office units occupied by physicians, lawyers, accountants, and other professionals—is spurring variety. Warehouse condos are also on the rise, as well as self-storage, marina, and airplane hangar condos. All of them share the same basic legal, financial, and social features as residential condos, but differ in the character of shared and private spaces.

Vacation Condos

Other than full-time residences, the vacation condo is the type most familiar to the largest number of people. These are projects at the beach, in the mountains, or on the lake—wherever people like to spend spare days or weeks. They can be very attractive as investments if you rent them out during the busiest seasons and reserve your personal usage to the off-season.

Vacation condo sales are currently fueling the building and selling frenzy going on in Florida and other hot areas. Investors buy contracts to purchase units not even built yet, and then flip those contracts for huge profits. While some of these markets may be cooling, there always seems

MYTHBUSTER

Vacation condos pay for themselves

It would be very unusual to make an operating profit on a vacation condo, so you should be prepared to subsidize the expenses, at least during the early years of ownership. Refer to Chapter 6 for more information.

to be another popular spot when the old one becomes unfashionable.

Vacation and second-home condos enjoy the same mortgage interest tax deduction as primary residences. You must pay taxes on any profit upon a sale, though, and cannot make use of the $250,000 ($500,000 for married couples) exclusion from income allowed for principal residences.

Kiddie Condos

Recently, student condos, commonly called *kiddie condos,* have emerged as a popular investment for parents with college-age children. To a lesser extent, student co-op apartments can also be found, but student town-home developments are extremely rare.

Rather than pay for a dorm room or rent an apartment, many families purchase condos for the duration of their children's stay at school, and then sell when the kids graduate. The projects usually have little to recommend them except for proximity to campus and perhaps some heightened security features. Recreational amenities are usually minimal or nonexistent. As a result, the resale market is limited primarily to other parents with college-age children.

Still, with reasonable appreciation, a condo purchase can prove much cheaper than other housing alternatives. Amazingly, the parents might actually earn an immediate profit on their child's college experience.

Game Day Condos

One of the hottest new trends is the *game day condo.* The game day condo is marketed to fans who want a place to stay during sporting events, without worrying about making reservations a year in advance at a hotel. For home games, they come to their own condo in their team's home city. Accommodations for out-of-town games are harder, but there is a lively market in game day condo rentals, just like vacation condo rentals.

Townhomes and co-ops are not really suited for the game day concept. The townhome owner must maintain his or her own lawn, worry about frozen pipes in the winter, and endure almost all the headaches of traditional home ownership. Sports fans do not want that—they want a parking spot, a place to sleep, and a party atmosphere. Co-operative apartment boards, who must approve new members before they are allowed to buy stock, are usually antagonistic to the concept of part-time residents with no emotional investment in the building and a party attitude.

Formerly, game day condo units were typically tiny, the sound-proofing nonexistent, and the appliances, plumbing, and carpeting were the cheapest possible—but owners were guaranteed a room for sold-out games. Today, wealthy sports boosters are willing to pay top prices for luxury surroundings, so the quality of game day condos is increasing dramatically. Beware, however, that these are sometimes truly the play-grounds of the rich. In college town game day condos, there is a movement among such projects to add restrictions against student occupants—even the children of the owners. For most of the year, the unit will sit vacant, while the expenses continue month after month.

Kosher Condos

Kosher condos are designed to meet the strict requirements of Conservative and Orthodox Jewish religious lifestyles. Units feature two dishwashers, separate countertops, and two sinks in order to allow religious Jews to cook and clean meat products separately from dairy products. Kosher condos will also typically have programmable timers that automatically turn lights on and off during the Sabbath in order to avoid the prohibitions against working. Most include a separate sink for ritual hand washing.

Leasehold Condos, Co-ops, and Townhomes

Leasehold CIDs are widespread in Hawaii and southern California, although they are also found in other parts of the country. They are developments built on land rented from someone else rather than owned by the developer. This is called a *ground lease*. It is strongly recommended that you not buy in such a development, but sometimes you may feel like you do not have any other options.

Likewise, sometimes the developer just does not have any other choice than to use a ground lease. In really great locations, like Hawaii, property owners typically do not want to sell their land. Developers cannot make a living unless they develop, but they might not be able to find any land to buy, so the parties execute a ground lease.

Even in less glamorous parts of the country, you sometimes see this arrangement. For example, it is often used when a charity, religious group, or school receives land by virtue of someone's last will and testament. Such gifts frequently contain restrictions forbidding the recipient from selling the land for fifteen to as much as ninety-nine years. Ground leases are a way to get around the problem and still earn some money.

In such arrangements, the developer leases the land, usually for ninety-nine years, and then builds a condominium, co-op, or townhome project. In all other respects, it is just like a typical development. The only difference is that the unit owners share rights in a long-term lease rather than rights in owned real estate.

At the end of the lease term, the buildings can all be bulldozed unless arrangements have been made to extend the lease or buy the land at that time. Most people buying during the initial twenty or forty years of a ninety-nine-year lease probably do not care, but at some point the property values will start declining dramatically, because new owners will be buying ownership rights that may die before they do. The right to live in a unit for the next twenty years is worth considerably less than the right to live in it for the next fifty years and then will it to the children. This is especially true for the majority of Americans who use their homes as their savings accounts—building up equity as the years go by, then converting to cash upon retirement or death.

Early owners should care about everyone making their monthly ground lease payments on time. If a few owners do not pay their monthly dues, and there is not enough money to pay the ground rent, then the other owners will have to ante up. Otherwise, the ground lease will go into default, and the landlord could terminate the lease and bulldoze everything immediately. Long before that happens, of course, lawyers will tie everything up, but lawyers do not work for free, so you end up between a rock and a hard place.

You should also be aware that it is much harder to obtain financing to buy a unit in a ground lease development than in other developments. Unlike automobile lenders, real estate lenders cannot get excited about the concept of collateral that gets less valuable with every passing year. Usually, the landlord must hold the financing. Current tax law provides some assistance on deductibility of the ground lease payments, but only in limited circumstances. On the other hand, you may also have the opportunity to live or vacation someplace that would otherwise be unattainable in your price range. This is a high-risk option, though, so fully investigate all your alternatives before choosing to buy.

Condotels

Condominium hotels, sometimes called *condotels*, are generally luxury developments containing furnished units. They are typically found in vacation and resort locations. One of the reasons they are so popular right now is that they are being marketed very heavily.

Someone who wants to build a resort can usually borrow only 50% of the money needed. One way around the problem is to sell off units to raise the other 50% of construction money. You, as an owner of one or more units, must agree to make your unit available for rental to hotel guests. The hotel, or a hotel management company, takes care of reservations, payment, cleaning, repairs and maintenance, and most other normal hotel responsibilities.

Condotels are popular with hotel developers, but they do have potential problems. One of the newest fads in class action litigation is to claim these arrangements are really *securities*. A security is defined by federal law as something that meets all three of the following requirements:

    1. a pooling of interests with others;

    2. an expectation of profit; and,

    3. passive management by the owner.

If something is a security, then federal law also imposes huge responsibilities on the people who sell it, and restrictions against things like insider trading. This is not just a problem for the hotel developer—it might also be a problem when you are ready to sell your unit. Further, if something is a security, you are now dealing with issues similar to those corporations must deal with when they sell stock on Wall Street, not just you trying to sell your condo in a simple real estate exchange on Main Street. Be sure to consult with an attorney or do some research if you are thinking about buying.

Limited Equity Condominiums and Co-ops

Limited equity condominiums and *limited equity co-ops* are forms of subsidized housing in which low-income consumers can qualify for ownership. Usually, nonprofit groups of lenders provide low interest rate financing for buyers. They are popular in the Northeast, particularly Washington, D.C. and Massachusetts.

Purchase prices are set at levels less than comparable units elsewhere. In exchange for an affordable purchase price, limited equity CID owners have to sell their units at reduced prices, and only to other qualified buyers with limited resources. Selling prices are determined by formulas that usually keep pace with general inflation, but do not take into account rapidly rising real estate prices in the general community.

A Style for Everyone

The preceding sections are just some of the different varieties of residential condos, townhomes, and cooperative apartments. There are even more projects that differ only in their *focus*—golf, tennis, snow sports, maritime, family, senior, assisted living, and so on. With such an incredible range of options, something will fit your needs exactly.

Your first question should be, "Am I ready to move from the traditional single home American dream of home ownership to something a little more restrictive but vastly more rewarding because of the value of cost-sharing?" By now, you probably already have a good idea of the answer. The next chapter helps you solidify your understanding of condo, townhome, and co-op life, so you will have no doubts at all about your decision.

Chapter 3:
The Condo Lifestyle

Almost this entire chapter applies equally to condo, townhome, or cooperative apartment living. To make things easier on you, all of these things are referred to by their generic name common interest developments (CIDs). If something in this chapter differs for each type of CID, it will be mentioned specifically.

Living in a CID offers virtually all the benefits of traditional home ownership. Mortgage interest is deductible, including the interest on a loan used to purchase stock in a cooperative apartment. Property taxes are deductible, including your pro rata share of the property taxes paid by a co-op building. Unit value usually appreciates over time. However, life in a CID also contains some of the same drawbacks as detached housing, such as large closing costs and market risks, and often regular maintenance expenses.

Common interest developments offer two extremely important advantages over typical stand-alone homes. First, they give you the ability to live in areas of extremely high real estate prices, where the price of the land alone would make residency impossible for most people. Second, they provide you with the privilege of enjoying amenities formerly reserved only for the very wealthy—full-time security, Olympic-size swimming pools, property management, perhaps even stables and riding rings, boat slips, private airfields, on-site day care, and many other benefits that would otherwise not be available to you.

Before going further, you should evaluate how much individuality you are willing to give up to gain the benefits you want. As a general rule, co-ops are the most restrictive, then condos, and townhomes last. There are variations of restrictiveness within each group, however. Decide early on the importance of the following issues to you, and then shop for something that fits your personality, not just your financial or other types of needs.

Are You Willing To Share?

Sharing expenses in order to get more expensive things also means you have to share the things. Problems come with all the *little* things you never thought you would have to share. For example, you might not have a particular parking place that is specifically designated for you. Someone might become irate if you hog your share of the dumpster by tossing in some old mattresses. Finally, think about possibly sharing bandwidth for your computer, hot water for your shower, or loading dock time for your movers. Are you okay with sharing these things?

Some things cannot be shared in a CID. There might be rules against burning incense because the other owners do not want to share your fragrances. Likewise, they might be opposed to the lovely melodies coming from your wind chime collection. You could be stunned to discover that the lighted Santa Claus who always sits in your living room window during the holidays is not welcome. Not only must you share many things, but you also must *refrain* from sharing many other things.

Can You Give Up a Little Control?

When living in a CID, owners have less control over their environment than with stand-alone dwellings. Your ability to modify your unit will usually be limited. Rules designed to prevent abuses by *other* people—self-centered maniacs bent on mayhem and destruction—might actually keep *you* from having a perfectly civilized, late-night party at the pool with fifty of your closest friends.

However, it is hard work making all the decisions that come with home ownership, and sometimes it is nice to have major decisions made for you by these rules. Isn't it okay if someone else picks out the carpet pattern in the hallways—even if it is a color you detest—as long as someone else also vacuums it every day? How terrible would it be if you could not paint your front door a beautiful shade of red, but your next door neighbor also could not paint his or her door some ghastly color like mauve?

By and large, members of a condominium association have the same interests as you. They want to share amenities on a reasonable basis, preserve property values, decrease the amount of time wasted on maintenance issues, and balance privacy concerns with the very human desire to build vibrant and interactive communities. Because people have widely different views about what is necessary to accomplish those goals, there have to be multiple rules rather than one golden rule. That is the heart of CID living.

Are you Willing to Participate?

In order to receive the full benefits of community ownership, you must be willing to take part in CID government. Folks who do not attend meetings or read the monthly newsletter will probably have unpleasant surprises ahead for them, because people who are vocal and who regularly review issues and vote on them will have the most influence on rules, regulations, and enforcement policies. Your ability to live happily and productively, with a minimum of objectionable restrictions, will depend on your input into the process.

Test: Is a Condo Right for Me?

To determine if condo living is right for you, try this quick test.

1. My privacy is:
___ Not important to me.
___ Somewhat important to me.
___ So important I used to be a hermit.

2. My need to be in control of my living environment can best be described as:
___ NOT a control freak.
___ Need to be in control, at least to some degree.
___ As a matter of fact, someone DID die and make me king.

3. Amenities such as swimming pools and tennis courts are:
___ Very important to me.
___ Not that important to me.
___ I'm not the athletic type.

4. I would respond to the following statement, "I like mowing the lawn, landscaping, and gardening," with:
___ Are you kidding?
___ I don't mind it.
___ I love working outdoors.

5. The following describes my position on doing my annual maintenance chores exactly on time:
___ I thought gutters flushed themselves out.
___ I am on top of it, give or take six months.
___ I have a laminated schedule taped on the refrigerator.

6. Home resale value is important to me:
___ Because I may be moving within the next three years.
___ But I expect to be here for a while.
___ Even though I plan to live here forever.

7. Living in an urban environment is:
___ Vibrant, exciting, and convenient.
___ Something I can either take or leave.
___ Not for me—give me the country life.

8. Meeting and interacting with many different types of people is:
___ Very important to me.
___ Relatively important.
___ I hate people.

Total all your points, giving yourself 1 point for each first answer, 2 points for each second answer, and 3 points for each third answer. Evaluate your scores as follows.

8 to 10 points:	Future president of condominium association
11 to 20 points:	A good candidate for CID life
21 to 24 points:	Thanks for buying the book anyway

Do not get discouraged if you scored in the 21 to 24 range but truly want to enjoy beachfront property part of the year, a retirement community that can adapt to your changing needs over time, or any of the other specialized CID opportunities.

Real estate developers understand market forces. They know that not everyone is a perfect CID candidate, but they still like to attract as many buyers as possible. If you shop carefully and do your research, you can find a community that is right for you.

Chapter 4:
Legal Overview

A good understanding of the legalities of ownership will help you recognize the importance of many of the steps explained later in this book. You will be able to conduct the right kinds of prepurchase property checks, recognize the signs of potential problems, and make the best buying decisions.

Despite the differences in condo, townhome, and co-op apartment lifestyles, CIDs still share some common legal considerations. Most of the laws relate to balancing the needs of the developer against the needs of the consumer purchasers, and to balancing the competing needs of different owners in the same community. This chapter answers questions you may ask about condo ownership, responsibility, and community living.

Specialized Law

Historically, property owners owned everything within their boundaries, to the center of the earth and to the top of the sky. Lawyers and real estate agents have about a thousand years of *common law*—recorded decisions by judges—to refer to for the answers to typical problems found with traditional detached housing. Condos are different because they slice up ownership in new ways, creating novel problems. Further, condos cannot exist except by virtue of condominium statutes passed in each state. When there is a dispute, people have to review the statute first for the answer. Fortunately, most of the statutes are similar to one another, even if they are somewhat different from old-fashioned real estate law. Fundamentally, though, condo law is real estate law.

Co-op law has a real estate component because of the landlord/tenant relationship between the owner and the corporation that owns the building, but not all disputes and procedures are determined according to those laws. There is also some corporate law, some Uniform Commercial Code law, and a growing body of specialized co-op law similar to nothing else. As if that were not confusing enough, some states replaced their old condominium statutes with newer common interest development statutes that also apply to co-ops.

A townhome, in its purest form, is just a matter of two properties sharing one wall, called a *party wall*. The law on party walls is pretty old and settled, and is considered traditional real estate law. However, most townhome developments include shared amenities, like green spaces or swimming pools, and have homeowners associations, which are kind of like corporations. All of these relationships, except for the actual party wall, depend on non-real estate law.

This is important because even if you are knowledgeable about real estate law, or have bought and sold many homes in the past, you cannot take anything for granted with a condo, townhome, or co-op apartment. Take the time to read the following sections, and you will be well rewarded.

Who Owns What?

The following chart recaps Chapter 1, showing ownership in condos, townhomes, and co-op apartments.

Who Owns What in a Condo, Townhome, or Co-op Development?

	CONDO	TOWNHOME	CO-OP
Rooms of the unit	You	You	The corporation
Doors and windows	Everyone	You	The corporation
Walls between units	Everyone	½ to each side	The corporation
Plumbing pipes	Everyone (usually)	You	The corporation
Faucets and tubs	You	You	The corporation
Electrical wiring	Everyone (usually)	You	The corporation
Light fixtures	You	You	The corporation
Recreational areas	Everyone	The homeowners association	The corporation

Remember that just because you and the other forty-nine members of your condo project all own the elevators, you cannot allow your children to ride on them all day long. There are rules, which vary from project to project, to prevent you from abusing your privileges in a shared environment.

Although you do not personally own any common areas all by yourself, you are usually given an exclusive right to enjoy some of them. For example, the balcony or patio to your condo unit is technically one of the common elements, but you alone will be given the right to sit there in the evenings and enjoy the sunset.

The condominium association is a governing body. It enforces rules, prepares budgets, collects dues, and manages the upkeep and repair of the common areas. The condominium association does not actually own anything at all—the unit owners all *share* the common elements. This is an important distinction when trying to figure out who has the right to contest property tax assessments on the common areas, who has the right to bring lawsuits against a developer for defective construction, and who gets sued when someone is injured in the common areas. Is it the association, or is it some or all of the individual owners? These are complex issues that change from state to state. Consult an attorney, call your state attorney general's office, or search the Internet. A good website to check out is **www.communityassociations.net/state_laws.html**.

In a townhome development, a separate association or corporation usually owns the common areas. Each owner is automatically a voting member of the association, and gets one vote per unit he or she owns. It used to be popular for the developer to keep recreational amenities and then lease them back to the association for huge monthly fees. Because of widespread financial abuses, however, this practice has largely been regulated out of existence.

A cooperative apartment is a corporation with shareholders and directors. It owns absolutely everything, including your unit. You buy stock in the corporation, which allows you to rent a particular unit. This is called a *proprietary lease*. The board of directors is usually rather picky about who will be allowed to buy stock, and thus rent a unit.

Once you are in, it does not mean you cannot be booted out, though. You can lose your lease, especially for repeated violations of the rules. In New York, for example, shareholders can terminate your lease if you engage in something the majority thinks is *objectionable conduct.* In one case, a tenant was obnoxious to his neighbors, spread rumors about some of them, started unauthorized repairs in his apartment, and was arrested twice for narcotics law violations. Even though the rent was paid on time every month, he was evicted. Courts in New York will not second-guess the shareholders on this issue; they are allowed to exercise their own *business judgment* and will not be overturned. That is why you see all those television shows and movies with apartment dwellers living in fear of offending the superintendent or the other neighbors. You do not really own anything at all with a co-op—not even the peace of mind that you can stay there forever if you want.

Who is Responsible for What?

As a general rule, remember that whoever owns something is responsible for it. In the case of a condo, all unit owners also own the common areas. Technically, everyone is responsible for upkeep, but the owners discharge their responsibilities by paying monthly dues and periodic assessments, and then leaving the details up to an elected board or officers. If the roof leaks just over your unit, then all the owners, through their monthly dues, pay to repair it—even though you are the only one affected by the water.

This state of affairs sounds attractive, but it can have some drawbacks. Suppose the roof leaks over just your unit. You want to climb up there and patch it, but the association decides to replace the entire roof, because the other owners think this leak is just the beginning of a lot of other problems. There is not enough money in the fund for such a large project, so they assess all the owners $500 each in order to install a new roof. You were willing to risk life and limb on a steep slope in order to make free repairs or put a bucket under the leak every time it rained, but you were outvoted and now have to ante up $500. That is life in a condominium project.

The other reason you must understand who owns what and who is responsible for what is because the one who is responsible is the one who is liable if something goes wrong. State laws vary widely on this subject, as do individual rules in different projects. In some circumstances, courts have decided that condo owners are personally liable if someone suffers an injury on common property because of some defect or dangerous condition. In other words, the condo association, as a separate entity, is not the responsible party—you are. You will have to satisfy any jury verdict by paying your pro rata share of the damages award. When in doubt about your potential liability, consult an attorney and maintain plenty of liability insurance.

You must also review the condo documents to discover maintenance responsibilities within the four walls of your unit (such as plumbing and wiring), plus the balconies and patios. If nothing is said on the subject, then each unit owner must maintain the items within his or her walls, and pay dues to keep up everything else.

Townhome owners generally share only a common wall. You owe each other the duty of supporting the wall, which means you cannot slice your side in half in order to make a room larger, because the remaining thin layer of wall would not be structurally sound anymore. Otherwise, each homeowner keeps up his or her own lawn, windows, roof, and landscaping.

Sometimes, townhome developments have shared areas, such as recreational facilities, streets, security gates, or waste water treatment plants. In this regard, they are no different from many subdivisions of traditional homes. A separate entity, like a corporation or nonprofit association, owns the common areas and is responsible for them. If someone is injured, the association is legally responsible, not the individual townhome owners. It is important for the homeowners association to have its own liability insurance and not rely on the policies of the individual owners. Otherwise, an injured party could sue the association, execute on any judgment, and seize all the recreational facilities.

Co-op owners will have the responsibilities spelled out in their leases, just like any other tenants. Usually, though, the lease contains some sort of open-ended clause that makes the tenant-shareholder responsible for *new or different* things not spelled out in the agreement. For example, building corporations might require all tenants to replace their old, inefficient appliances with modern, energy-efficient ones in order to decrease the power bills each month. If allowed under the legal documents everyone signed, this will become a new responsibility. Otherwise, co-op maintenance and repair is entirely the responsibility of the corporation that owns the building.

How Much Independence Do You Have?

In a shared environment, there are always restrictions. Some can be more severe than others. At a minimum, you will not be allowed to personalize the exterior of your unit. You may be limited in number, size, or type of pets. The ability to have live-in help or extended-stay houseguests might be strictly controlled if there are prohibitions against nonfamily members living with you. Vacation condos sometimes require *dead weeks* when you cannot rent your unit—times when maintenance and repairs can be performed without worrying about complaining tenants.

It is always important to read the bylaws and the rules in order to discover written restrictions, but do not stop there. There might be a move afoot to add more, so you should also read the association minutes for the prior twelve months. Besides alerting you to potential problems, this will also give you a feel for community politics. You will develop a feel for the identity of the perennial complainers, the team players, and the leaders.

This is important, because peer pressure can be a strong consideration. Even if there is nothing specific about it, associations can exert pressure to curb certain cooking styles using strong spices, excessive frying, or smelly vegetables. They might frown on weeknight parties, outdoor grilling, or children running up and down hallways. If you take the time to visit with the perpetual complainers, you will find out much about the unwritten rules of a condominium, townhome, or co-op apartment community.

Legally, only the written rules can be enforced through a system of penalties or fines. In the typical situation, the association will issue written warnings to noncompliant

MYTHBUSTER

Comprehensive rules will help maintain property values

Most people think that lengthy written rules will keep property values high and neighborhood relationships tension-free. In reality, if the rules have not been enforced in the past, then a court will usually deny you the right to enforce them in the future. The more detailed the rules, the more likely it is that they will not *all* be enforced by owners, negating any benefit of having the rules in the first place.

owners. Failure to come into line can result in monetary fines, which if not paid, could escalate to court action or even foreclosure on the unit. Do not be frightened by the story on page 29 about co-ops and objectionable behavior. While that seems pretty vague, your protection is that the shareholders must give you some sort of notice about what is objectionable and an opportunity to shape up before they ship you out.

The courts tend to side with CIDs and against individuals on issues regarding rules violations and fines, as long as there has been consistency in enforcement. If you are unhappy, judges and juries will tell you that you agreed to the rules and regulations when you bought your unit. As long as the rules are not discriminatory, vague, or capable of more than one interpretation, they will be upheld.

Owners' Constitutional Rights

In years past, CIDs justified comprehensive restrictions with their desire to maintain uniformity and with the owner's real or imputed knowledge that this was going to be the case. The argument was that the owner knew what he or she was getting into when the unit was purchased, so there was no complaining about a situation. Courts sided with the associations. Today, the climate is changing, perhaps because this type of ownership is becoming so widespread.

One of the major battlegrounds of owners' rights has always been the ability to express one's political views by placing signs in windows or on lawns outside units. Almost always, the association or the board was successful in preventing these displays, because of rules prohibiting such activity. However, in February of 2006, a New Jersey court made a landmark decision, saying homeowners are entitled to certain state constitutional protections, such as freedom of speech. This was despite the association's argument that recognizing constitutional rights would "create chaos, erode private property rights, limit the freedom to contract, discourage new development, cause associations to lose their flexibility, and infringe the rights of the majority." If you are interested, you might want to read the whole decision by looking up *Committee for a Better Twin Rivers v. Twin Rivers Homeowners' Association*, a New Jersey case. It is expected to be appealed, but could mark a change in owners' rights.

Typical Condominium Rules

Developments vary in some of the details of their rules, but there are some recurring patterns. The most common rules follow.

- *Unit maintenance.* Owners cannot allow their units to fall into disrepair and possibly damage other owners. An example might be plumbing leaks that could result in toxic mold. Water beds are usually prohibited.

- *Unit decoration.* There are generally strict guidelines regarding holiday decorations and length of time they can be displayed, and stern warnings against customized landscaping, painting, trim, and even drapery linings.

- *Exterior usage.* You cannot set up a clothesline on your balcony for drying beach towels. Many developments also prohibit outdoor grilling, portable fireplaces, wind chimes, and fountains.

- *Occupancy.* Some condos restrict occupancy to residents over the age of 55 (this is a legal exception to the Fair Housing Act). Others limit the total number of occupants, or the number of nonfamily occupants. There may be exceptions for live-in caregivers, but there might not.

- *Residence use only.* There are probably restrictions on home-based businesses. Even if you provide only consulting services, receive no visitors, produce no products, and store no merchandise, you could still be required to obtain another address for your official business address. Fortunately, telephone answering and mail handling services are common and inexpensive these days, so this should not be too much of a burden.

- *Pets.* Even in garden home condo communities, where each unit has a backyard, pets usually must be kept inside. It is common for associations to limit the size and type of pets to no dogs or cats over twenty pounds; no birds except for canaries and parakeets; no fish tanks over fifty gallons; and, no reptiles, amphibians, insects, or other animals at all.

- *Visitor registration.* Visitors spending more than one night must usually register with the association, its management company, or security. It is generally recognized that communities that monitor their guests suffer less crime than those that are more lax.

◆ *Vehicle size, type, and number restrictions.* Because of scarce parking, you may be allowed to keep only one vehicle at a time at the facility. Off-site parking will have to accommodate your other cars. There will usually be limits on the size of trucks and outright prohibitions against boats, trailers, and motor homes. Inoperable vehicles, or even vehicles that cannot be legally operated on public streets due to lack of inspection stickers, cannot be kept at most condo projects.

◆ *Vehicle registration.* Numbered parking decals help identify strange vehicles and assist with security. In addition, when you register your vehicle, you give the association an early opportunity to advise you if it is nonconforming. Some associations charge an *impact fee* based on the number of vehicles you have registered.

◆ *Lease terms.* If you are an investor, you might be forced to offer leases no less than one year in length, in order to cut down on turnover. Generally speaking, you will be responsible if your tenants fail to follow the rules. There may be a charge each time tenants move in or out, because of the additional wear and tear moving places on corridor walls and carpets, the usage burdens on the elevators, and the parking problems caused by moving trucks.

◆ *Tenant registration.* If you rent your unit to others, you may be required to furnish extensive information about your tenants and the terms of their leases. This is for security, accountability, and maintenance of standards. You may think it is your own business if you want to rent out your luxury condo to a student for $300 per month, but it could seriously impact other unit values. In addition, any fees for background checks on potential tenants will be charged to you—not billed to the association.

◆ *Signs.* "For Sale" or "For Rent" signs are usually not allowed. If they are, the association has severe restrictions on the size, type, number, and colors. Political signs might or might not be allowed, and this restriction might or might not be enforceable under state laws protecting free speech.

Owners who do not follow the rules usually have fines assessed against them. If the fines are not paid, they become a *lien* against the unit. Technically, unpaid liens can lead to foreclosure and loss of the unit. As a practical matter, the fines usually pile up for several years until a sale, when they will have to be paid out of any sale proceeds.

Sometimes, a condo association will go to court and request an *injunction* (court order) forcing the owner to obey the rules. If there is an injunction in place, then failure to comply can result in jail time for contempt of court. While all of this sounds pretty scary, it can give great comfort to other condo owners that rules will indeed be enforced, property values preserved, and all neighbors allowed to live together in peace and harmony.

Typical Townhome and Co-op Rules

Townhomes are basically just like subdivisions, except for the shared wall between two units. You will usually see normal subdivision rules, like restrictions on noise during certain hours, prohibitions against inoperable vehicles anywhere but a closed garage, and perhaps limits on size, timing, and lighting of holiday decorations. There might be an architectural review committee that must approve exterior renovations for stylistic consistency with the rest of the neighborhood. If there are amenities—such as pools, tennis courts, and common party rooms—then there will be rules for their usage. Otherwise, you enjoy a great deal of independence.

Co-op apartments are concerned with the same things as condo associations—preservation of property values and keeping peace among neighbors in close quarters. As a result, they have most of the same rules as condos. There may be some additional ones required by life in New York City, where co-ops are so common. Many co-op rules address concerns over tenant interaction with building employees, most of whom belong to unions. Great care is taken to protect the rights of the union employees, and to make sure nothing happens that causes a walkout. In addition, it is simply not that easy to stop a moving truck outside a building in New York City. Move-ins and move-outs must be scheduled far in advance in a co-op.

Finally, you should remember that a cooperative apartment building almost always has a master mortgage to some lender, who must be kept happy through adherence to rules. As an example, the lender might require that all tenants provide proof of liability insurance in a certain amount. If the building suffers an uninsured loss that decreases its value, and the whole thing is really *your* fault, the lender can sue you and recover from your insurance company.

Ignoring the rules in a townhome development usually has about the same consequences as in a condo. Co-op boards, on the other hand, have the very drastic remedy of canceling your lease. Courts will usually side with the co-op boards if they have followed all the technicalities properly, unless the tenant can prove that lease cancellation was a result of fraud or other sinister motives.

What if the Condo Developer has Financial Problems?

If the developer runs into financial problems and lets the bank take over the project, what you end up owning may be far different from what you thought you were buying. Unfortunately, there may be little you can do about the situation, but you should have some understanding about the risks involved and how the situation could play out.

For most new condo projects, the developer will initially take *reservations* in order to evaluate market interest. If enough people pay a deposit for reservations, the developer will go ahead and build. If not, all deposits are refunded and the project will not go forward. Assuming market demand is strong, the developer will then presell some units at below-market prices in order to quickly raise cash for construction. The balance of the construction money is provided by lenders, who take mortgages on the project. As each unit is sold, the lender will release its mortgage on just that unit, but keep it on everything still owned by the developer.

Problems arise if the developer cannot complete the project or cannot sell all its remaining units. Three things can happen at that point—construction gets shoddier as corners are cut, some amenities are not completed, or the lender forecloses on the project. In that instance, what are your rights? Individual owners still own their units, subject only to their own personal mortgages, but the lender is now a co-owner in the common areas, and probably has a majority of the votes in the association. That is because every unsold unit still owned by the developer, and then foreclosed by the lender, represents a vote—one per unit. In most states, the developer owes *fiduciary duties*—an extremely high degree of responsibility—to unit owners. The lender, after it forecloses, usually has no such restrictions. Their goals are different from your goals.

As an example, what if the recreational amenities are incomplete? If the developer had a *performance and completion bond*, then the lender could force that bonding company to complete the project. (In the real world, a defaulting developer has usually done something to cause the cancellation of the bond, as well.) Banks usually have very short-term planning horizons regarding foreclosed real estate. They are not interested in completing projects now, just to make more money in the future selling their units over time.

Unsold units on which the bank foreclosed will be dumped on the market at greatly discounted prices. If you are trying to sell or refinance your unit at the same time, that could spell bad news for you. It could also change the entire feel of the project. The original price structure, for example, might have been suitable for high-income, two-earner couples with no children. Drastic price reductions could attract families with young children. What was once an exercise pool will become a children's play area. The elegant circular driveway will have school buses parked in it several times a day, because it is much safer than stopping on the street. These are all great things for families, but not what you bargained for when you bought your unit.

What if a Co-op Board has Financial Trouble?

It is not unusual for co-op tenants to turn management over to whoever is willing to take the job, and then forget about supervision. More expensive buildings generally hire third-party management companies and outside accountants for auditors. Co-op boards trying to economize in order to keep rents low might rely on the services of a volunteer shareholder or an unsupervised professional manager. That person or group can go for years with little or no oversight. All the tenants pay their rent on time and assume the building's taxes, utilities, insurance, and mortgage payments are also being made on time. Sometimes, that trust is misplaced and the manager has either embezzled the money or simply not handled it prudently, resulting in delinquencies. The tenants first learn of impending disaster when the problem reaches crisis proportions—with threatened foreclosure or utility disconnection.

If discovered early enough, the tenants might be able to borrow money to cure any tax or utility defaults. They can negotiate with the building lender to extend the term of the note, but even if successful, they will incur attorney's fees and loan expenses. Insurance policy cancellations might go unnoticed until there is a loss, in which case it will be too late to fix the problem.

In all these instances, the tenants have no real rights, even though they have paid hundreds of thousands of dollars for their residences. All could be gone in the blink of an eye, with no true recourse, because they are only tenants. The best defense against such dire possibilities is to buy in a well-managed building, stay involved in supervision, attend all shareholder and tenant meetings, and review the financial records on a regular basis.

While all of these legal considerations are important and could seriously affect your ownership rights, most of the potential horror stories will, fortunately, never happen. Social and political issues, on the other hand, are much more common, and capable of affecting your every day life. Some of the most important considerations are covered in the next chapter.

Chapter 5:
Social and Political Considerations

The true fabric of any society is made up of relationships among people, and the written and unwritten rules that govern their interactions. It is the same in a village, a private club, a family, and a common interest development. This chapter helps you understand some of those processes and rules, so you will be prepared to make intelligent choices from among the many options available to you.

Condo Government

The condo association is the financial and enforcement mechanism for the owners. All condo owners are automatically members of the association, although they may elect an executive committee, officers, board of directors, or some other vehicle for routine decisions. Owners have one vote for each unit they own or some percentage based on the size of their individual unit. In the beginning, when the developer still owns most of the units, he or she will also have most of the votes. State laws prevent the developer from using its voting strength to push through changes that would damage the other owners.

In the beginning, the developer appoints all directors, who hold office until the first regular meeting of the condo owners. The Bylaws set out the frequency of meetings and elections, as well as the procedure to be followed for electing new directors or officers. They also establish certain standing committees, such as for oversight of recreational facilities, enforcement of rules, and management of finances. In a large project, with numerous directors, the Bylaws may provide for an executive committee empowered to make certain routine decisions without input from the other directors or owners.

Usually, there is a light turnout at the regular association meetings, unless something dramatic is on the agenda. Association meetings are generally boring—the same people complain about the same things. However, buried in there somewhere between the reading of last month's minutes and the request for volunteers to supply refreshments at the next meeting, you will find lots of important business being conducted.

If you are going to live in or invest in a condo, you should schedule time to attend the monthly meetings in person or by proxy. A *proxy* is someone who has your permission to cast your vote. A *general proxy* authorizes someone to vote on any association business coming up at the meeting, in whatever way he or she thinks best. A *limited proxy* requires him or her to vote in a particular way on specified issues only. For the most part, only limited proxies are allowed for condo association meetings. In order for your proxy to be effective, you must make sure to comply with any technical requirements for proxy votes. The Bylaws will have those requirements.

A condo community is a democracy, but there are varying rules about the size of the majority (number of votes) required for different decisions. Usually, anything that decreases the common elements will require a unanimous vote. Proposals to materially change the common elements or amend the Bylaws will need some type of *supermajority*—usually 75%. Other decisions and election of officers generally require only a simple majority. The general rule is the more dramatic the change, the more votes necessary to make it.

If you believe that some issue or election has been improperly decided, you may either go to the courts to obtain an injunction, or submit the matter to binding arbitration. The modern trend is for condo Bylaws to require arbitration rather than submission to the courts.

Strong leadership in the association can do much to preserve property values and enhance the quality of life. It can also micromanage all the residents into mutiny and flight. Weak or complacent leadership probably will not start expensive new projects every year, but it might also allow problems to fester until they become crises. When making a buying choice, be sure to factor into your decision the dynamics of the condo association, and how that fits with your particular philosophy about controls and restrictions.

The Homeowners Association

Townhome communities usually have a homeowners association that owns any shared recreational facilities, plus perhaps some green areas, an entrance sign, and the fencing, gates, and roads (if it is a gated community). It will be run by officers who are elected from time to time, as specified in the Bylaws.

Like condo associations, there will usually be some *standing committees* to oversee things like maintenance, finances, and rules enforcement. A standing committee is established in the Bylaws, and remains in existence for the duration of the association unless the Bylaws are amended. Members serve for specified periods of time. As a practical matter, the same people usually serve on the same committees, year after year, because no one else wants the job. While this certainly promotes efficiency and a high level of expertise, it can also lead to stagnation, mismanagement, and sometimes abuses. It is a good idea to volunteer for committee work and change committees every several years.

One of the most important committees in a townhome development is the one devoted to architectural review. Because townhome residents own their buildings, including the façade (outside front), they generally feel entitled to make any changes they want. Someone in a community of red brick Georgian townhomes might become bored with all the sameness, and desire to paint his or her brick white. Someone else might want to dig up his or her manicured front lawn and install a Japanese rock garden. There is nothing inherently wrong with these decisions, but they do destroy the integrated look and feel of the neighborhood. Some people view these kinds of change as a bad thing. Frequently, homeowners will be prohibited from making any changes to the exterior of their property unless an architectural review board approves them. This is probably one of the greatest areas of strife in a townhome community, and leads to the most hard feelings and lawsuits—even fistfights.

Ad hoc committees are formed to address particular problems. Once the problem is solved, the committee disbands itself. Examples would be a committee to contest property tax increases, one to petition the city for speed bumps in the neighborhood, or maybe one to make recommendations for changing the Bylaws.

Because of the greater degree of ownership and control over individual space afforded owners of townhomes, their homeowners associations are usually much less intrusive than condo association boards.

The Cooperative Board

As with any other corporation, the stockholders of a cooperative apartment project elect a board of directors to the run the corporation. The co-op board of directors exercises much greater control than a condominium owners' association, because the co-op owns absolutely everything in the building, including your unit. If you do not comply with the rules in a condo or townhome development, those associations can impose fines on you. If you are willing to pay the fines, you can pretty much keep doing what you have been doing. The consequences of rebellion in a co-op are much more severe. Depending on the details of the bylaws, a board might be able to cancel your lease if the members are unhappy with you or your visitors.

In the past, cooperative apartments were very successful in discriminating against certain classes of people, such as minorities, families with young children, and single women. The discrimination was made easier by the board's ability to approve or disapprove tenants. Now such activities are illegal, but boards still have a great deal of leeway in rejecting tenants for other reasons.

Noise

If it has been a long time since you lived in an apartment or dorm, you have probably forgotten about the importance of noise considerations. It is the number one source of problems in condos, townhomes, and co-ops. In all probability, you will be surrounded by people—above, below, to the left, and to the right. You might be a quiet person who reads in the evenings, so it would not occur to you that others might be avid and vocal fans of wrestling matches, stock car races, or opera music. Some people cannot even walk quietly from room to room, but instead seem to stomp their way through life.

Urban dwellers might also have traffic, elevated railway, and construction noise to contend with. Garbage trucks arrive at the crack of dawn. Older buildings sometimes contain creaking elevators, gurgling pipes, and rumbling heating systems. Many people cannot deal with that, and need to concentrate their search on newer buildings with ample soundproofing and quiet systems. Others can simply tune out the world at will.

It is not uncommon for there to be very little insulation between units in an older apartment project converted to condos or co-ops, or in older townhomes. Local fire and safety regulations may have required fire-rated walls, but the typical two-hour rated fire wall consists of two pieces of ⅝-inch thick wallboard. More upscale developments sometimes provide acoustical insulation, but not always. The good news is, newer projects in hurricane-prone areas generally have so much concrete in them that you could not hear an anvil drop on your ceiling.

If peace, quiet, and privacy are important to you, then you should ask the appropriate questions or conduct some self-tests. Visit the development during busy times of the day—mornings before work, afternoons after school, and evenings during television prime time. (You will need to clear this with building security, the real estate agent, or the seller, so no one thinks you are trespassing.) This exercise will tell you a lot about noise levels in the building and about neighbor sensitivity to the privacy of others.

If you want some sound control, but cannot afford or cannot

INSIDER TIP:

To test your noise tolerance, buy a CD with some type of music you cannot stand, like opera, hard rock, hip-hop, or country/western. Play it for several hours while you do other things. If possible, have a friend increase the sound level for short bursts at unexpected times. Can you soldier through, unfazed, or does this drive you to distraction? The answer will tell you how much emphasis to place on noise control issues. If you are easily distracted, your budget may dictate smaller, well-insulated units, rather than huge lofts of wide open space with thin walls.

find the quality you need, here are some pointers. Hardwood floors are beautiful but noisy. Some buildings require area rugs on all floors, and some do not. End units are more quiet than interior units, unless there is construction on the next lot. The closer you are to the elevator, the more traffic there will be in the hallway outside your door. Master bedrooms are usually on the end and have windows, but the smaller, interior bedroom will be the most peaceful at night.

Your ear will hear what is closest to it, so you can sometimes mask exterior noise with fountains, soft music, or an aquarium. Hang tapestries or rugs on the walls to muffle sounds from other units. Position bookcases along the walls between units, not along interior walls. If space allows, you can position bookcases by the front door to create a small alcove to block hallway noises. Buy insulated draperies, which provide very effective thermal and sound insulation, and usually come with either white or black linings. (You will need to see if there are restrictions on types of window coverings.) Buy the thickest rugs you can afford. If your budget permits only flea market purchases, splurge on really thick carpet pads, or find several rugs and layer them. One couple tacked insulation to their ceiling, and then disguised it by hanging yards of fabric from the ceiling for an exotic effect in the bedroom—romantic and practical.

In short, while noise is the number one complaint in CIDs, it is usually the one problem most easily solved with a little planning. As always, think ahead and you will avoid most of the unpleasantness that can mar your home-owning pleasure.

Privacy

Aside from noise intrusion, other factors might impact your sense of privacy in a condo or co-op development. Higher security usually results in decreased privacy. Continuously monitored security cameras, if available, could be a good thing or a bad thing, depending on your point of view. Electronic access to common areas via card-key or even biometrics (retinal scan or fingerprints) helps exclude intruders, but it also generates a report of your comings and goings. A building Internet server with built-in firewalls could provide low-cost, state-of-the-art telecommunications and constantly updated child-safety filters—but it could also allow an unscrupulous administrator to view all the Internet sites you visit and to monitor your emails. Some laundry rooms can send you an email when your washer finishes its cycle, but that also means someone can access reports regarding how often you do the laundry.

Buildings seem to develop their own personalities over time. Some are huge, bustling neighborhoods where someone is always dropping in to borrow sugar or discuss last night's game. Others are exceptionally discreet, with neighbors never even making eye contact in the elevators. Think about your personality style when choosing a place to live. The best way to test the waters in an established building is to ask the seller about his or her neighbors. You will start to get the flavor of the community pretty quickly.

Remember, sharing results in greater benefits without paying greater prices, and this results in some loss of privacy. Evaluate how you feel about this before buying.

Developments with Residents of Similar Interests

For many people, the choice of housing location hinges on important community considerations. Some cater to families with young children, providing play areas with closed-circuit television, on-site day care, and even small commissaries with convenience store items. If you want your children to have a large pool of potential playmates close to home, then you probably want to choose such a project.

You may be more interested in a diverse group of mature adults with whom to make friends, play cards, take ballroom dancing lessons, or travel to exotic locations. The highest concentration of such people will probably be in projects that target such an age group—ones near good health care, convenient to a number of leisure activities, and containing a minimum of child care amenities.

If you keep your particular age and lifestyle requirements in mind when shopping for a condo, you will improve the odds of your ultimate satisfaction with your choice.

Other people recommend against buying in a development with people of similar interests. They say you should buy in an area where there is as much diversity as possible. It exposes you to a wider variety of people with whom to form relationships. It also helps ensure that whatever peculiarities you have will be better tolerated. Senior citizens rearing their grandchildren might do better in a diverse community than in a complex consisting of only retirees or only families. When it comes time to sell, there is certainly a wider potential pool of purchasers if you live in a mixed-personality development. The downside is that you are competing for buyers against every other mixed-personality development in your area.

There is no right answer here. Determine your needs and philosophies, and choose accordingly.

Chapter 6:
Deciding What You Can Afford

If you start out defining the perfect condo with all the truly wonderful amenities you might ever need or want, and then turn your attention to budgeting, you tend to buy more than you can afford. That is the danger of emotionally committing to certain features before you evaluate their relative cost.

According to the National Association of Realtors, median condo prices outstripped median detached home prices in the fourth quarter of 2005, for the first time in history. During the three-month period from October to December of that year, the vast majority of homes purchased were in the neighborhood of $213,000. At the same time, most condos cost $228,200.

To see how much home you can buy for various prices, visit **www.bankrate.com** and search the site for the word "condo." You will find a report, complete with slide show photographs of actual properties. In the same general market area, comparing traditional housing with similar condos, the condo will generally be slightly more expensive per square foot if the real estate market is stable. That is because you are buying more than just your own square footage when you buy a condo—you are also buying access to all of the common areas and amenities.

It is important to remember this if you are moving from traditional housing into some type of CID. If you have outgrown your 800-square-foot cottage—financially and spatially—then you might start shopping for a 1,500-square-foot condo, townhome, or cooperative apartment. In reality, however, your budget might not permit something that large. Do not wait until you submit your loan application to discover this—do your homework first. You may be pleasantly surprised to discover your budget covers only 1,200 square feet, but that is all you need.

Make truly informed decisions by budgeting first and shopping second. Salespeople would rather you did it the other way around. They work on commission, so the more you spend, the more they make. It is not a question of ethics, but more a matter of rosy optimism tinged with enlightened self-interest. The real estate agent truly believes you can afford all the extras you want, and is not going to question your judgment if you agree. Unfortunately, bankers are not much better at offering you realistic numbers. Traditional bankers do not get commissions, but they do get bonuses based on production levels, and mortgage brokers do receive commissions. What is good for them is not necessarily good for you.

MYTHBUSTER

If I prequalify for a loan, that is how much I can afford to spend

Never forget that lenders are in the business of renting money to you. They will stretch in order to justify loaning you as much money as possible. Underwriting calculations regarding what you can afford each month might assume you never eat out, never buy clothing, will not want any new furniture or accessories, that you are always healthy, will never need any repairs, take public transportation to work, and live on about six hundred calories a day. Just because your lender is willing for you to have an impoverished lifestyle in luxury surroundings does not mean you should go along with the idea.

Some real estate experts tell you to buy more than you can afford, and then grow into the property, financially speaking. That sounds nice, but consider what a precarious position this puts you in. One hiccup in the economy, one instance when you fail to get a raise you were counting on, or one totally unexpected major expense like a new refrigerator, could drive you into bankruptcy if you are already living right on the edge of your financial resources. Preparing a housing budget is the first step to finding the perfect, stress-free home.

Working Up a Housing Budget

Buying a CID should not reduce your living standard to that of college freshman on a limited scholarship. What you want to determine is how much you can afford without experiencing a drastic reduction in your lifestyle. This is actually pretty easy to do. First, calculate your average monthly nonhousing expenses. Then, subtract this sum from your monthly after-tax income to find the amount available for housing.

If you use computer banking or household budgeting and bill-paying software, it will take only a few minutes to complete the exercise. For those less computer-inclined, go through your checkbook and monthly credit card invoices to get a good idea of how you spend your money. A six-month review should be more than enough. Use the monthly budget worksheet found on page 52.

To complete the worksheet for calculating the monthly housing expense you can afford, follow these steps.

◆ Start with your monthly after-tax, take-home income, as it is today. If you are expecting a raise, you can account for that later in the worksheet.

◆ List your *recurring expenses* by category for the last few months. Recurring expenses include things like car payments, school loans, orthodontist visits, private school tuition, day care, piano lessons, charitable or religious donations, health insurance, credit card payments, alimony or child support payments, and an estimate for food, cleaning supplies, and toiletries. Do not include utilities right now.

◆ Make a separate list of big ticket, infrequent expenses, such as life insurance premiums, auto insurance, vacations, gift-giving, and so on. Do not include homeowners insurance or renters insurance, because these will change with your new residence. Total all of these items and then divide by twelve to find your monthly *reserve expense*. It is wise to make sure you have these funds set aside so that you do not end up running large monthly deficits when these expenses come due. This monthly reserve expense gets added to your budget of regular monthly expenses.

◆ Separate your credit card bills by type of expense. These might be things like gas, restaurants, entertainment, clothing, laundry, pet care, and impulse purchases. Resist the urge to reform yourself by promising you will never, ever visit eBay again. This reform will not happen, so you should allow for some of those purchases in your budget. Add all these credit card expenses up for the last six months and then divide by six to obtain a monthly average. These are your *periodic expenses*—they do not have a regular schedule, but they do come up in varying amounts every month. Add this number to your budget.

◆ Review your check register for all the cash withdrawn from ATM machines or checks you have cashed. This is probably your money for things like mid-morning cappuccinos, magazines, and movie tickets. Add up these cash expenses for the last six months and then divide by six to obtain a monthly average. Add this number to your budget.

◆ The worksheet assumes you have payroll deductions for some sort of a retirement plan, so these deductions are not included in this budget. What you should include, though, is a small amount each month to build up a cushion in the event of job loss or slowdown. Financial planners suggest you have at least three months of living expenses in savings, but six months would be better. Now, while you are shopping for a new home, is the best time to start good habits of saving.

◆ Total all these monthly nonhousing expenses.

◆ Assess the difference between your take-home pay and the expenses you calculated above. If the difference is large, where does the money go each month? You may have forgotten to include some expenses in your budget, or there may be some expenses you will no longer have with your new condo or co-op. After all, someone else will have to worry about lawn maintenance, snow removal, gutter cleaning, exterior painting, brick cleaning, and all the other joys of suburban home ownership.

◆ Make adjustments upwards or downwards depending on what you think the future will look like. Will you get a raise? Will the children need braces in the coming year? If you get a promotion and a raise, will you be expected to join a private club, entertain more often, buy a new car, or dress better? All of these will increase your expenses and eat away at the increased pay.

◆ Can you legitimately reduce some of your nonessential spending? Be reasonable here. Vowing to live on canned goods for the next year, rather than occasionally dining out, is not realistic. Make the necessary adjustments. Subtract the total from your take-home income. This leaves funds available for your new unit.

Calculating the Monthly Housing Expense You Can Afford

	AVERAGE COST PER MONTH	ANTICIPATED INCREASES OR DECREASES	NEW HOME EXPENSES
Monthly After-Tax Income			
Recurring Expenses			
Health Insurance			
Car Payments			
Health Care			
Education			
Charity/Religious Organizations			
Club Dues			
Alimony			
Child Support			
Other:			
Reserve for Annual Expenses			
Average Periodic Expenses			
Average Miscellaneous Cash			
Savings and Investments			
Other:			
Other:			
Other:			
Other:			
Total Monthly Expenses			
Funds Available for Housing			

It is from the "Funds Available for Housing" row that you will pay your mortgage payments, monthly dues, utilities, property taxes, and hazard insurance. This will, in turn, set a limit on the maximum price you can pay for a condo, townhome, or co-op.

Preapproved Loan Amounts

The most important factors that lenders look at when making loan decisions are credit score, employment history, and net worth—in that order. Only then do they evaluate how much of your income must be devoted to housing costs. Those financing guidelines will determine whether you get the loan, how large a loan you receive, and what the interest rate and origination fees will be.

To determine the maximum purchase price they think you can afford, lenders compare *PITI* (principal, interest, taxes, and insurance for a proposed home loan) to your monthly income. The traditional rule was that PITI could not exceed 28% of your monthly take-home pay. In other words, if your take-home pay was $5,000 a month, PITI could not exceed $1,400 a month. If debt service, taxes, and insurance exceeded this number, you would not qualify for a loan.

Some lenders use a different formula and include utilities and other loan obligations in their calculations. The ratio they rely on says that PITI plus utilities and installment debt cannot exceed 36% of monthly take-home pay. *Installment debt* is any debt that has more than ten or twelve

MYTHBUSTER

Lenders want to save you from paperwork

Although this is mostly true, sometimes it is for the benefit of the lenders. Many mortgage brokers will tell you not to fill out the monthly expense section of a loan application. They say they can save you time, and will simply pull that information from your credit history. The problem is that the credit reporting agency may show your car loan and your credit card expenses, but it might not show alimony payments, child support, or student loans. The broker is actually hoping that some monthly expenses do not show up, so you will qualify, on paper, for a larger loan than is truly prudent for you. Contrary to popular belief, lenders and brokers are huge optimists, and desperately want to believe that you can make things work.

months (depending on the lender) of payments left to make—such as a car note or student loan. If you have a car payment, but the car will be paid off in ten months, lenders do not count it. One of the shortcomings of this approach is related to the installment debt issue. Just because your car is going to be paid off in ten months does not mean you are not going to buy a new car at the end of that time. You might still have installment debt, but it will not be included by the banker when he or she calculates how much mortgage you could afford.

To make matters worse, the growing use of automated underwriting and credit scoring means that even the faulty ratio calculations are applied very loosely. It is not uncommon for loans to be approved with much higher cost-to-income ratios than the traditional 28% or 36%. What lenders place most emphasis on now is job stability and credit history. In other words, they will decide that if you have a good credit score, it means you are a responsible person. The thinking is that responsible people are willing to live on hot dogs for the next five years in order to afford a more expensive home. It is an unrealistic system, but that is how it works.

Dues and Assessments in Condos and Townhomes

Your evaluation of what you can afford should not stop with the monthly mortgage payments. Just because a CID development is advertised as "worry-free" does not mean it is actually "dollar-free" regarding maintenance and other headaches.

While it is certainly nice to have the benefit of a swimming pool, tennis courts, a maintenance person, and a security guard, these things all cost money on an ongoing basis. In addition, just because you are not responsible for replacing the roof when it ages does not mean that a new one magically appears when needed. Remember, too, that it is a thankless task to manage association finances, shop for the best prices for repairs, audit all the bills, and reconcile the association checkbook. Most associations hire a third-party management firm to handle those tasks and to ensure firm and continuous enforcement of the Bylaws. If you are not willing to do the management duties for free, rest assured that no one else will either. Management fees add to the monthly expenses.

Association expenses break down into two categories—maintenance and capital expenditures. Generally, routine maintenance and upkeep expenses are covered through monthly dues collected from each unit owner. Large *capital expenditures*, like roof replacement, parking lot resurfacing, and other such things, are handled two different ways. Some associations like to build up a *reserve fund* over time. If a new roof for a twenty-unit building will cost $45,000, and the association thinks a new one will be necessary in fifteen years, the association might start collecting money each month so it is available in the future. Leaving aside the issues of inflation versus money growth through interest, in order to have $45,000 in fifteen years, the association will need to collect an extra $12.50 per month per unit in order to be ready. (Divide $45,000 among twenty owners to get $2,250 per owner. To have that at the end of fifteen years, each owner needs to pay $150 per year, or an extra $12.50 per month.)

The other method of dealing with the problem of future expenditures is to wait until the future and then assess all the owners their pro rata share. In other words, keep the monthly fees low, but in fifteen years make everyone ante up an extra $2,250 to pay for the roof.

Each system has its supporters and detractors. You should evaluate how you feel about the subject and then shop for a property with a similar philosophy. It is all well and good to adopt a *think about it tomorrow* attitude to capital expenses—unless the project is fourteen years old when you buy, and it is time for a new roof. On the other hand, if you plan to buy a condo as a short-term investment, you want the monthly dues as low as possible, and will let future owners worry about replacing the roof.

Generally speaking, condominium projects composed primarily of owner-residents will have slightly higher monthly fees in order to keep sufficient reserves on hand. Developments pitched as starter homes, investment opportunities for resale, or vacation dwellings will have smaller monthly fees with a Russian roulette attitude towards capital expenditures—"maybe they will be needed while I'm an owner, or maybe I'll dodge that bullet." Townhomes rarely have large repair or replacement expenses because the associations do not own very much.

Many brand-new condos still under the control of the developer will have extremely low monthly dues in order to attract buyers. Beware of this *bait and switch* tactic, because the association budget may not allow for things unnecessary in the first year, but essential afterwards. For example, the new elevators and building systems (plumbing, heating, etc.) will initially be under warranty. Future years will require maintenance contracts that will become increasingly expensive as time passes. New landscaping will not suffer any plant deaths, but subsequent years may see large recurring expenses in that area. Some maintenance items may be ignored completely because they will not show up until later.

If you think you will be on a fairly tight budget, you will not be able to afford any assessment surprises. You want to look for something brand-new with a realistic maintenance budget, or a community that collects slightly higher monthly dues but builds up a reserve for capital expenses.

Co-op Rent and Maintenance

Co-op apartments do not have dues like condos and townhomes, but you will have to pay rent or maintenance each month. This figure can vary widely within the same general area. The building corporation will have to pay its mortgage, utilities, maintenance expenses, and payroll. The money to do that can come from several sources—your monthly rent or maintenance payments, interest earned on cash reserves, profits made by sub-metering utilities and re-billing to the tenants, impact fees for moving in or out, rent for parking places or single-room *maid's quarters*, and any *flip taxes* imposed by the building when units are sold.

Higher rent might mean more things are included in the rent. Lower monthly fees might mean that more things are paid in other ways. Once you work up your budget, you will have to ask lots of questions to make sure any particular co-op building will allow you to live within that budget.

Converting Housing Budget to Purchase Price

Once you know how much you have available to cover monthly housing-related expenses, it is a relatively simple matter to determine the prices of homes that are within your budget. Use the worksheet on page 57 to determine your purchase price.

Purchase Price Worksheet (with Examples)

	CONDO EXAMPLE	CO-OP EXAMPLE	YOUR WORKSHEET
Monthly Income Available for Housing	+ 2,500	+ 2,500	
Monthly Property Taxes	- 208	- 0	
Monthly Insurance	- 100	- 50	
Monthly Fees	- 250	- 718	
Monthly Utilities	- 210	- 0	
Total $ for Monthly Debt	= 1,732	= 1,732	
Funds for Down Payment	30,000	30,000	
Interest Rate	7%	7%	
Maximum Purchase Price			

Ask an insurance agent what the average insurance premium would be for a home in the general price range you think you can afford. For co-op buyers, you will need to price specialized co-op insurance to cover all your personal belongings and the interior of your apartment. You can call the local tax assessor's office to find out how much the property and school taxes would be for a unit in the price range and general area of town you desire. Utility expenses for co-ops might vary from building to building—some buildings pay the entire bill, others sub-meter and re-bill the tenants at cheaper rates than generally available, and still others have individual utility meters at each apartment.

You figure out maximum purchase price by using some of the numbers from the worksheet on page 57, plus something called a *monthly loan constant*, and then doing a little simple arithmetic. A monthly loan constant is a number you use that acts as a shortcut for a lot of other math calculations. The table on page 59 gives you the monthly loan constant for different interest rates for a thirty-year loan. If you want a different loan term, ask a banker or a mortgage broker to give you the monthly loan constants you need. After you have the correct monthly loan constant, you can figure out your maximum purchase price.

MYTHBUSTER

For similar sizes,
utility bills will be comparable

This is not a clear-cut issue. Picturesque condos or co-ops in older buildings are probably not as well insulated as the house or apartment you currently occupy. You might have to increase your utility budget. Top floor units usually enjoy cheaper heating costs and more expensive cooling costs because heat rises, and because of the greater number of hours of direct sunshine coming in the windows. Also, if you are moving from the Sunbelt to the North, you will find that winter heating expenses will be more expensive than the summer cooling expenses you are used to. That is because, in the summer in the South, you must reduce your home temperature by about twenty degrees under the outside temperature in order to be comfortable. In the winter in the North, you must increase your home temperature by about forty to sixty degrees above the outside temperature in order to be comfortable. That is much more expensive.

Monthly Loan Constants for a Thirty-Year Mortgage Loan

Interest Rate	Constant	Interest Rate	Constant
5.00%	0.00537	7.50%	0.00699
5.25%	0.00552	7.75%	0.00716
5.50%	0.00568	8.00%	0.00734
5.75%	0.00584	8.25%	0.00751
6.00%	0.00600	8.50%	0.00769
6.25%	0.00616	8.75%	0.00787
6.50%	0.00632	9.00%	0.00805
6.75%	0.00649	9.25%	0.00823
7.00%	0.00665	9.50%	0.00841
7.25%	0.00682	9.75%	0.00859

Instructions	Example	Your Numbers
Take "Funds for Down Payment" and multiply by the Monthly Loan Constant for your interest rate (7% in our example)	$30,000 x 0.00665 = $199.50	
Add that number to "Total $$ for Monthly Debt"	$199.50 + $1,732.00 = $1,931.50	
Take that number and divide it by the Monthly Loan Constant for the interest rate (7% in example)	$1,931.50 ÷ 0.00665 = $290,451	
Maximum Purchase Price	**$290,451**	

You can also visit any number of websites that will perform the same calculations for you. One such website, **www.cheapskatemonthly.com**, also includes other useful budgeting and financial calculators.

Mortgage Interest Tax Deduction

If you are currently paying rent, the tax consequences of mortgage payments could affect your decision making. The Internal Revenue Service (IRS) allows you to deduct home mortgage interest from your income in order to arrive at something called the *adjusted gross income* (AGI). You actually pay taxes only on the AGI.

There are some limits on the deductibility of home mortgage interest. Currently, only the interest on $1,000,000 worth of mortgage debt is deductible, so if you are planning to buy a $1,500,000 condo with 20% down, then your mortgage will be $1,200,000. Only part of your interest will be tax deductible—the part attributable to $1,000,000.

Home equity line of credit interest is deductible on only $100,000 worth of debt. You can have more debt that that, but only the interest on the $100,000 portion can be deducted. Second home interest is deductible. However, your combined mortgage debt is limited to that $1,000,000 ceiling.

Co-op owners may deduct the interest on any loan used to buy stock in the building, and their pro rata share of the interest on the master building mortgage, subject to the same limits as other homes. However, the corporation itself must fit within certain IRS requirements to qualify. Among other things, the building corporation must receive at least 80% of its income each year from the tenant-stockholders rather than from earnings on investments. You can read the details in IRS Publication 936, "Home Mortgage Interest Deduction." For more information on the mechanics and details of home ownership deductions in general, refer to IRS Publication 530, "Tax Information For First-Time Homeowners." You can download these from the Web at **www.irs.gov/publications**, or you can call 800-TAX-FORM.

Your tax savings will depend on how much interest you are going to pay and what tax bracket you are in. Tax brackets are based on your filing status (married, single, etc.) and your adjusted gross income level. The brackets are prorated (as your income increases, the percentage of tax on each additional dollar increases), so even if you are in a higher tax bracket, part of your income is still taxed at the lower percentages.

Example:

Say you are in the 28% tax bracket, making $120,000 per year, and your mortgage interest deduction will be $24,000 per year. Will you save 28% of $24,000 ($6,720)? No. In reality, that number is too high, because of what is called *climbing the brackets*. If you make $120,000, then some of the income is taxed at 10%, some at 15%, some at 25% and only a very small amount—$50—at 28%. Your savings will be only $5,987.50.

The chart on page 59 helps you calculate your first year's interest and the tax savings on that interest. It is only an estimate. The better practice is to have a mortgage lender prepare an amortization schedule for you for the loan amount and terms you think you will be able to obtain. You can also go on the Internet to any number of websites that will do the same thing for you, such as **www.bankrate.com**, **www.ditech.com**, or **www.quickenloans.com**.

Calculate Home Mortgage Tax Deduction Savings

Instructions	Example	Your Numbers
Use your calculations from page 59 for the amount of condo you can afford. Enter that number here.	$290,451	
Enter the amount of down payment.	- $30,000	
Subtract the down payment from the purchase price.	= $260,451	
This is the amount you will finance.	$260,451	
Enter the interest rate you think you will have.	7%	
Convert the interest percentage to a decimal by dividing it by 100. You can have more than two numbers to the right of the decimal (ex: 6.25% = 0.0625).	7 ÷ 100 = 0.07	
Multiply the decimal interest rate times the amount you will be financing.	260,451 x 0.07 = $18,231	
This number is an estimate of the mortgage interest you will be paying in your first year.	**$18,231**	
Use the IRS tax tables to obtain your marginal tax rate. (Go to **www.irs.gov** for the tables.) Multiply that by the interest number above. The number you calculate will be a little bit higher than your real tax savings.	$5,104 (assuming you are in the 15% tax bracket)	

NOTE: *If your income is close to a tax bracket change, use the lower rate.*

The number in the last box will be your *approximate* tax savings because of the mortgage interest tax deduction.

Those who are already homeowners probably should not count on any additional tax savings. Your take-home pay, in all likelihood, already takes into account the mortgage tax deduction. If you want to figure out how much a higher payment will save you in taxes, then you are planning to squeeze every last penny out of your calculations in order to figure out how much house you can afford. That is not a good idea, because you are tying to justify more house than you can truly support. Be conservative in your calculations. If you cannot find anything in your price range, then you can try being a little more aggressive by figuring areas where you can economize. It is always a bad idea to juggle the tax numbers.

Special Considerations for Co-ops

When you buy a co-op apartment, you are really only buying stock in a corporation that owns a building. You will then be *allowed* to pay monthly rent and occupy a particular unit. The calculations regarding what you can afford sometimes get very complicated. You might be able to pay a huge amount for the stock if you have really low monthly rent payments. If the rent is gigantic, you might tolerate only a very small purchase price. It makes it difficult to calculate the purchase price you can afford to pay. If you are working with a real estate professional, tell him or her the monthly amount you can afford to pay, and he or she will know which combinations of purchase price and rent will meet your budget. Those of you scanning the classifieds or the online listings will need to do a lot more calculations as you make your calls.

Vacation Rental Income

Many people buy vacation condos and count on peak season rental income so the unit will *pay for itself*. The ability to do this is largely a myth—unless you are very self-sufficient, resourceful, and energetic—because a lot of expenses will eat away at your profits from rentals.

Management expenses can typically run from 10% to 20% of the gross rent. That is on top of things like expenses for advertising, background checks, and credit card processing fees. Your unit will require more frequent cleaning and maintenance, because renters simply are not going to take care of it as well as you do. They will also turn the air conditioner down to sixty degrees and leave all the windows and doors open, allow toilets to run, and do other things to drive up your utility expenses.

You can self-manage, handle your own bookings and payments, advertise on the Internet, and arrange for freelance cleaning and repair services, but this is a lot of work. Think twice before taking on such responsibilities. Be sure to buy a good book on the subject. One such book is *How a Second Home Can Be Your Best Investment,* by Tom Kelly and John Tuccillo.

Hidden extra costs can include impact fees charged by your facility, charges for the association's own approval process and background check, and rental taxes imposed by local governments. These things will all be deductible expenses on your taxes, but you will also have to report your rental income and pay taxes on it.

Overall Financial Analysis

For most people, living in a condo, townhome, or cooperative apartment can be a way to economically enjoy a wide variety of services and amenities not otherwise affordable. You should do your financial homework. If it makes sense for you, then do it. Do not let fear of the unknown financial territory keep you from making a decision.

Chapter 7:
Financing Options

There is a dizzying variety of financing options that allow people to enjoy the American dream of home ownership. In order to navigate them successfully, and make the most economical choice with the least risk, you need to know about:

- different types of lenders;
- the importance of credit scores;
- how the *secondary market* affects underwriting;
- important loan terms; and,
- common traps to avoid.

By the end of this chapter and the next one, you will have mastered all these areas and be armed with the tools you need to confidently shop for and negotiate the best loan terms possible.

Overview of Mortgage Lending

Most mortgage loans come from one of the following sources:

- conventional loans:
  - banks;
  - mortgage companies;
  - brokers;
  - savings banks; and,
  - credit unions or

♦ government-sponsored guarantees or loans:
  ♦ Federal Housing Administration (FHA);
  ♦ U.S. Department of Veterans Affairs (VA); and,
  ♦ Rural Housing Services (RHS).

The common expressions *conforming* and *nonconforming* are used to describe whether or not the loans follow guidelines set by Fannie Mae and Freddie Mac. To further complicate the vocabulary, almost all loans are *originated* one place—the primary market—and then sold to others in the *secondary market.*

The two largest purchasers of home loans on the secondary market are Fannie Mae and Freddie Mac. Although they do not directly loan any money to borrowers, their strength as buyers allows them to effectively set the underwriting requirements for mortgage loans. That is because they will not buy any loans that do not meet their guidelines. Lenders need to sell their loans, so they will have more cash to loan out on more mortgages.

The largest single family loan Fannie Mae will buy is $417,000, with some exceptions for particular geographic areas. For Freddie Mac, the limit is $359,650. Anything larger cannot be bundled into the standard resale packages. This is important to you because you can generally receive cheaper interest rates if you qualify for a Fannie Mae or Freddie Mac resale of your loan. If you are slightly over the top loan limits, you might want to pay a slightly larger down payment in order to come within the requirements. Larger loans, often called *jumbo loans* or *nonconforming loans*, are usually kept in the lender's private portfolio or charged slightly higher interest rates and sold to other types of investors. There is nothing derogatory about a nonconforming loan.

Shop for Financing Early

After you have figured out what you can afford, it is time to shop for financing. Do this before you make any offers. While you can put a *financing contingency* in any offer, which lets you cancel a contract without loss of your earnest money if you cannot get a loan for some reason, in really hot markets, sellers will not allow you a financing contingency. In less frenzied parts of the country, it always adds a psychological edge to your negotiations if you are able to say with confidence, "We do not need a financing contingency." Sometimes, you will be able to bargain the price down a few thousand dollars if the contract does not depend on your getting loan approval afterwards. Finally, after you have found your dream home is not time to start shopping for financing—you will want to be shopping for furniture and accessories. Comparing rates, fees, and terms will be critical to determining how much money you will have left over for these home furnishings, so it is an important first step.

Know Your Credit Score

Home mortgage lenders have a wide variety of underwriting standards when evaluating your loan application. While most lenders will allow payment-to-income ratios well above the old 28% and 36% guidelines, credit scores have become the single most important factor in loan approval. Scores of 650 or more will qualify you for the best interest rates. A score of 750 or above is considered excellent, while 800 or above is a stellar credit rating. The higher your score, the more leeway you will be given if you do not meet other underwriting guidelines for income, job stability, or loan-to-value ratios. Do not give up if your score is under 650—you can always take steps to improve it, or you can find financing from a lender that specializes in what is called *B-paper* or *B loans* (as in A-quality, B-quality, etc.). The interest rates will be higher and the fees will usually be larger, but you can qualify for a loan.

If you do not know your credit score, contact all of the three consumer credit rating companies—Equifax, TransUnion, and Experian—and request a copy of your report. The reason you want to obtain all three is because different lenders use different reporting agencies, and some use a combined report from all three. They do not always carry the same information or assign the same scores as each other. By law, all three agencies must give you one free credit report per year, but you can request, and pay for, more than one. For details, go to **www.annualcreditreport.com** or call 877-322-8228. You can also write to:

Annual Credit Report Request Service
P.O. Box 105283
Atlanta, GA 30348

Improving Your Credit Score

There is nothing magic about a credit score—it is just the number that pops out of a computer after running all your information through a formula that a fallible human being invented. The formula itself is complicated, changes frequently in its minor details, and is guarded with the same ferocity as secret service agents protecting the president. Yes, it can be flawed in its application to your case, or the data the computer considers could be in error. If you clean up the errors and work on putting things in the best possible light to fit well within the formulas, then you will improve your score significantly. Remember, though, it is a computer. You cannot argue with it, you cannot explain your special circumstances, and you cannot beg for a score of 649 to be upgraded to a 650.

It seems that the ideal person—according to the credit scoring computer—has no more than two bank cards, with small balances charged and then paid off monthly. Still good, but less than perfect, is if your balance is no more than 50% of the high limit allowed, and more than the minimum payment is made each month. The cards should be old ones, with no evidence of constantly getting new cards to pay off old ones. All reported bills should be paid on time. There should be very few credit inquiries—meaning you are not constantly applying for department store credit cards that promise instant discounts if you are approved. Inquiries can deduct as much as five points each from your score. (Your personal inquiries, or those from existing creditors, do not count against your score.)

If you have old credit accounts, such as gas cards, department store cards, home equity lines of credit, and so on, but never use them, you show fiscal restraint. Closing the accounts shows that you might not trust

---

MYTHBUSTER

*Paying off all my debt
will improve my score*

Credit scores depend on evaluating how well you pay your bills on time, month after month. If you come into a windfall and pay everything down to $0 balances, that does not say much about how you pay your monthly bills. Resist the urge to act quickly and pay off credit card balances. Instead, be patient for several months and pay them down in large, but regular, payments. It will have a lot more impact on your score.

yourself. Keeping them open, but never using them, will make you the darling of the credit scoring computer.

If there are mistakes on your credit report, you can contest them and have them deleted. The information might be completely wrong, or it might be so old that the law requires it to be deleted regardless of whether it is correct.

The rules for how long information can be reported can be found in the Federal Code, at 15 U.S.C. Sec. 1681, or online at the website of the Government Printing Office, at **www.gpoaccess.gov/uscode**. (Enter "15usc1681c" in the search box under "2000 Edition, Supplement 2.") According to law, the following items cannot be reported, and must be deleted if you contest them:

- ◆ civil suits, civil judgments, or arrest records older than ten years or the statute of limitations, whichever is longer;
- ◆ paid tax liens older than seven years (credit reporting bureaus and the Federal Trade Commission (FTC), which administers these rules, take the position that *unpaid* tax liens can be reported forever);
- ◆ accounts placed for collection more than seven years ago (when in doubt, the FTC assumes that an account will be placed for collection 180 days after it first becomes delinquent); and,
- ◆ anything else, other than crimes, older than seven years.

An important exception allows reporting of older information if the consumer is applying for a loan of $150,000 or more, life insurance with a face value of $150,000 or more, or a job with an annual salary of $75,000 or more.

Each credit reporting agency has its own procedure for contesting information. As a general matter, upon receipt of your dispute, the agency will send a written inquiry to the credit reporter to verify the information. If the adverse credit information is not confirmed within thirty days, it must be deleted.

You can speed things up if you are reaching a deadline for a loan closing. You will have to speak to a customer service representative at the reporting agency in order to get an expedited handling, and you will need to tell them you have a closing scheduled within forty-eight hours.

Services that charge you a fee to clean up your credit usually rely on the fact that a lot of bad credit confirmation inquiries get lost in the shuffle. In other words, the credit grantor never answers its mail in order to verify your particular information. It is not legal or ethical to take advantage of this, but a certain percentage of credit grantors will simply not get around to confirming perfectly accurate bad credit. If unconfirmed after you have contested it, the information must be deleted. Be aware, though, that it can appear again at a later date. Most credit information reaches the reporting agencies via electronic data tapes that automatically dump data into the computers. You will need to check your credit report frequently if you are relying on the timely deletion of bad information—but remember that each report after the one free annual report requires a fee.

Less than Perfect Credit

If you get your credit score as high as you think will be possible, and the score is still low, do not despair. First, make copies of your final credit reports and the scores, and start visiting with mortgage brokers and lenders in your area. You do not want to actually complete any applications at this point, because each time a prospective creditor checks your report, it lowers your score. Remember, though, that lenders are in the business of lending money. It is an extremely competitive business. The lenders are highly motivated to sit down, work with you, and figure something out.

As a general rule, direct lenders such as local banks or credit unions can be more flexible than mortgage brokers, because mortgage brokers (including online brokers) must rely on processing large numbers of loans that fit within certain preestablished underwriting requirements. Brokers might have access to loan programs with less stringent requirements, but they will not be able to talk to a decision maker who can be persuaded to take a chance on you. Direct lenders can do that, because they keep some loans for their own portfolios and do not sell them on the secondary market.

You have to visit with more than one lender or broker—at least three or four—because there have been some widespread abuses in the industry. Some brokers will not tell you that you qualify for a lower interest rate with one company, but a high rate with another company. They will make you think that your credit is so awful, only the high-interest rate company will approve you. Some lenders pay loan originators a *yield spread premium*—a bonus based on a borrower agreeing to pay a higher-than-market interest rate. When disclosed to the borrower, this practice can have legitimate purposes, such as a borrower agreeing to higher interest rates in order to reduce up-front fees or down payment requirements. Still, you should shop around to avoid fraudulent broker practices.

Even with a terrible credit score, you can still obtain financing and an affordable interest rate if you can do some additional things. Finding someone with good credit to guarantee your loan, or a portion of it, will usually help. Also, the more money you pay as a down payment, the less risky the lender views the loan. If you live in a small community and work with a local lender, and if you have a stable work history, you can sometimes work out a payroll deduction for mortgage payments. Do not be afraid to ask lenders, "What would it take for you to make this loan?"

Some people have huge assets in cash or stocks, but just do not pay their bills on time. It is a lot more common than you would ever believe. If you fit into that category, almost any lender will be happy to finance your purchase, so do not be bashful about asking.

Lenders grade borrower quality and their loans as "A," "B," "C," or "D." A loans meet the creditworthiness requirements dictated by the largest purchasers of home loans, Fannie Mae and Freddie Mac. Many commercial lenders specialize in B, C, or D loans. They should be used as a temporary solution until you can increase your credit score enough to qualify for a conforming loan with lower interest rates. Following is a table showing the effects of increasing your credit score and refinancing as soon as possible. The example uses a purchase price of $120,000, with $25,000 down payment and a $95,000 loan, for the different interest rates and terms.

Comparison of Loan Interest Rates and Terms

	12% INTEREST	7% INTEREST	7% INTEREST
Loan term	30 years	12 years	30 years
Monthly payments	$977.18	$976.96	$632.04
Total interest paid	$256,784.80	$45,682.23	$132,534.40

As you can see, if you can lower your interest rate but keep your monthly payments the same, you could pay off your loan in twelve short years instead of thirty, and save over $200,000 in interest. That is why it is so important to continue working on your credit score, even after approved for a mortgage, if you want to later qualify for a conforming loan.

Points

Borrowers typically pay *points* in connection with a mortgage loan. One point is equal to one percent of the loan, so a fee of one point on a $150,000 loan would be $1,500. The money can be used for a wide variety of things, so it is important to find out the purpose of the points, as well as the amount, when comparing loans. There are two varieties—*origination points* and *discount points*. Origination points cover closing expenses and fees, including the mortgage broker's profit. Many of the fees covered by origination points are really just disguised additional profit for the broker or the lender, and are completely negotiable. Discount points are used to *buy down* your interest rate because you are prepaying some of the interest with the discount points.

How much you can reduce your interest rate varies with the type of loan and market conditions at the time. Typically, though, you will have to make mortgage payments for several years before you start saving money because of the buy-down. You will need to evaluate how long you will own your home to see if discount points make sense for you.

Example:

Suppose you want to borrow $100,000 on a thirty-year, fixed-rate mortgage. You think you can get a 7% interest rate with no discount points, or you can save one quarter of a percent if you pay one point. The one discount point will cost you $1,000.

Monthly payment @ 7.00%	$665.30
Monthly payment @ 6.75%	$648.60
Monthly savings	$ 16.70

At a savings of $16.70 per month, it will take you 59.88 months, or almost exactly five years, to save enough money to reimburse yourself for the $1,000 paid in points. Will you be in the home that long? Probably not. This is just one of the many ways lenders make money from unwary borrowers.

Common Lender Traps

Theoretically, mortgage brokers shop the market in order to find the best deal for you. Sometimes it does not actually work that way, and the broker is looking out for its best interests, not yours. Loan officers can also be guilty of sharp practices, downright fraud, or simple laziness—even though it might not directly benefit them. Beware of both groups, keep your eyes open, and question everything. The following are a few examples of lender traps.

   ◆ *Bait and switch rates.* The broker or lender quotes one rate, but once you are too deeply committed to back out, tells you something has happened and you are no longer eligible for the cheap interest. As a general rule, if someone quotes a rate that is 0.5% lower than anyone else's deal with comparable terms, then it is probably too good to be true. Ask for written quotes and the underwriting requirements to qualify for that rate. In addition, obtain a written estimate of all fees and third-party expenses you will have to pay in connection with the loan. Discounted interest rates could be more than offset by extremely high up-front fees.

◆ *No-fee loans with hidden fees.* Sometimes lenders will pay the origination points on a loan, so the borrower does not have to pay them. These are then advertised as *no-fee* loans, but they are really *zero points* loans. The fees for various things such as credit review, underwriting analysis, flood zone verification, and so on can be substantial. By federal law, some or all of such fees must be treated as additional interest for purposes of calculating the Truth In Lending figure called the *annual percentage rate* (APR). This is different from the *face rate* on the note, which is the rate usually quoted to you in sales pitches. When shopping, ask for a written estimate of the APR for the size and term loan you are requesting. If the APR is substantially higher than the quoted interest rate, then there are some fees you should know about before making any decisions.

◆ *The disappearing rate lock.* Most brokers and lenders will commit to a certain interest rate for a short period of time. If the loan does not close within that time, your rate could go up. You can agree to pay additional fees or points and lock your interest rate for a longer period. Even if interest rates rise in the meantime, you still get the benefit of your locked rate, assuming you close on time. Some dishonest brokers charge you the lock fee, but then keep the money rather than paying the actual lender in order to lock the rate. They are gambling that rates will not increase in the meantime. If you obtain a lock, ask for written confirmation from the actual lender, not from the mortgage broker.

◆ *Interest rates that do not drop with the market.* If you are quoted one rate and then, before you lock, the market increases, you will have to pay the higher interest rate. On the other hand, if interest rates fall in the time between your application and your lock, some lenders and brokers will not tell you. They will just let you pay the higher-than-market interest rate, unless you challenge it. Do not quit tracking interest rates once you put in an application.

◆ *Interest rates that increase to an artificial market.* You might receive a quote for a low interest rate that will increase to market after a period of time. The problem is, loan documents might define market as something artificial and completely within the control of the lender, no matter what the rest of the United States is doing. Lenders can make the market—and your interest rate—whatever they want. The thing that defines the market is called the *index*. At the time of your loan application, the lender should disclose to you what index it will be using. Commonly acceptable ones are Constant Maturity Treasury (CMT), Treasury Bill (T-Bill), 12-Month Treasury Average (MTA), and London Interbank Offered Rate (LIBOR). If your index is not on this list, investigate further. There are many other reputable ones—too many for this short section.

◆ *Fake expenses.* You may encounter a great variety of fees for things such as underwriting, document preparation, credit review, appraisal review, and other such things that are really just additional profit to the broker or lender. These are completely negotiable and can be waived if you insist. The federal government does not have hard and fast rules about what fees must be treated as interest for purposes of calculating the APR, and lenders have some leeway regarding what to include. Just because you ask for an estimated APR and it turns out to be very close to the quoted interest rate does not mean there will not be a lot of lender fees at closing. Always ask for a list of expenses, a good faith estimate of the amount, and a statement regarding whether they are paid to the lender, the broker, or an independent third party.

◆ *Borrowers with less than perfect credit pay very high interest rates.* You usually know if your credit is not perfect. You are psychologically prepared to be turned down for financing, or to pay a higher interest rate than other people. Brokers sometimes take advantage of this by quoting you a higher rate than the one you actually qualify for. The broker receives a fee based on the difference between the interest you should be paying and the rate you agreed to—the *yield spread premium*. Used properly, the yield spread premium compensates the broker for services he or she provides to you, and can also be used by the broker to fund certain closing costs that might be too expensive for you. In other words, you might agree to pay a higher interest rate in order to not have any closing costs. Used improperly, the practice amounts to price gouging and is predatory. Almost every state has class action litigation going on over undisclosed yield spread premiums. To protect yourself, ask how the broker will be paid and what amount. Remember, loan brokers do need to make a living, and not all fees are suspect.

Prepayment Penalties

Some loans contain provisions that require you to pay a penalty if you pay the loan off earlier than agreed or make larger principal reductions than the lender planned. If there is a penalty, it is generally only during the first few years of the loan. Sometimes it is a percentage of the loan balance at that time, and other times it is six to twelve months' interest. The reasoning is that a lender counts on receiving an income stream for a certain period of time. If the lender receives principal early, then the lender must loan it to someone else as quickly as possible. That might not happen immediately, and it will almost certainly require some marketing and administrative expenses.

Fully Amortizing Loans

Fully amortizing means that the regular monthly payments will eventually pay the loan, in full, over a specified amount of time. This is the most common type of mortgage loan today. Thirty-year terms are the most widespread, although some longer terms are making an appearance. Many people urge shorter loan terms in order to save interest. Over the course of thirty years, a $100,000 mortgage at 6% interest will result in $115,838 in interest, with payments of $599.55 per month. For the recommended twenty-year term, total interest drops to $71,943, but payments increase to $716.43 per month.

On the other hand, most Americans keep their homes less than ten years. So, as a practical matter, the property is sold and the loan is paid off long before the completion of the term.

Balloon Loans

Balloon mortgages allow a fixed interest rate, giving you stability in your financial affairs, but the entire loan will be due in five or seven years. Because the lender's potential exposure to below-market rates on your loan is limited in time, it can offer you somewhat lower rates than might otherwise be possible on a thirty-year mortgage. Many times, you have the option to *convert* the loan to a regular mortgage at the market rate for thirty-year loans, *plus* a little bit of extra interest, usually ⅜ of a percent. If you have a five-year balloon with a conversion option, the loan is called a *5/25 Convertible.* For seven-year balloons, it is called a *7/23 Convertible.*

Adjustable-Rate Mortgages (ARMs)

Adjustable-rate mortgages (ARMs) or *variable rate loans* initially have a lower interest rate than fixed-rate mortgages, by about 0.5%–1%. The difference on a $100,000, thirty-year mortgage, at 5% instead of 6%, is about $60 per month. For some buyers, this amount can make the difference in whether they can afford a home or not, or what size home they can qualify for.

The downside of an ARM is that the rate changes every so often—usually one, three, or five years, but it can be more frequent. The time interval during which it must remain unchanged is called the *adjustment period.* At the end of an adjustment period, the rate can increase or decrease, depending on what is happening with interest rates nationwide.

Any time you obtain an ARM loan, you should know the maximum amount the rate can increase in any year (*periodic cap*), and the most it can increase, totally, during the term of the loan (*overall cap*). Most commonly, an ARM has a limit of 1% per year increases, and the rate can never be more than 5% higher than the initial one. Although common, they are not required. Be sure to ask lots of questions about caps. By law, almost all adjustable-rate mortgages must have an overall cap in some amount.

Some ARM loans have *payment caps*, meaning your monthly payment cannot increase above a certain amount, even if the interest rate rises sharply. This is common with mortgages that do not have periodic caps, only overall caps. The danger is something called *negative amortization.*

Suppose your payment cap is $500 per month, but your interest rate increase should have resulted in a payment of $550 per month. Your lender does not just forgive the extra $50 in interest—your lender takes that $50 per month out of your equity. Rather than amortizing your loan so the principal balance gets lower each month, you are negatively amortizing and your principal balance is getting higher every month.

It is common for ARM loans to offer really low initial rates, called *discounted rates*, combined with large points or initial loan fees. Very large discounts are usually arranged by the seller of a property, who pays your lender a fee in order to obtain a lower interest rate for you. Payment sticker shock could set in when the rate increases to market, which could be 2% to 3% in additional interest.

Convertible ARMs are adjustable-rate mortgages that can be converted to fixed-rate mortgages at your option. There is usually a fee for the conversion, so you should find out the amount before you agree to the loan.

Interest-Only Loans

Many lenders have been aggressively marketing *interest-only loans*. The upside for the borrower is that monthly interest payments are as low as possible. Lenders like this, because more people qualify for loans based on mortgage-payment-to-income ratios required by underwriters. The downside is that the loan balance does not decrease, and there is usually a balloon or a conversion to full amortization in five to ten years. In order to be successful, the arrangement absolutely depends on real estate prices increasing steadily every year, so you can sell or refinance when the balloon comes due. In the alternative, with the conversion type of interest-only loan, you must be financially capable, in the future, of making payments on what will essentially be a twenty-year loan instead of a thirty-year loan. To clarify, if you have a thirty-year interest-only mortgage with a ten-year conversion, you will not make any principal reductions for the first ten years. Beginning in the eleventh year, you will have to begin paying down the loan, so that it is paid off in the remaining twenty years of the term. This will result in substantially higher payments. For a $250,000 mortgage at 6% interest, the monthly payments for the first ten years will be only $1,250. For the next twenty years, they will be $1,791.08 per month.

Most financial planners caution against interest-only mortgage loans. You have a risk of foreclosure if the market takes a downturn, your neighborhood declines in value, or your earnings do not increase substantially over the years so you can afford the much higher payments. Traditionally, the arrangement made sense for people with a small monthly income supplemented by large periodic bonuses or commissions they could use to pay down principal. It was also popular for affluent borrowers when the stock market was at its height. Wealthy borrowers would take the money they saved on monthly payments, invest it in stocks, and earn 15% to 20% on their funds. At the end of each year, they would sell some stock, pay down the mortgage balance, and pocket the profit. This is not recommended—this is just how it used to work.

For most Americans, the savings on an interest-only mortgage are simply not worth the risk. Monthly payments on a $250,000 interest-only loan at 6% interest are $1,250. After three years of the interest-only loan, you will have built up no additional equity in your home. The same loan, fully amortizing over thirty years, results in monthly payments of $1,498, and you will have paid off almost $10,000 of your loan after three years.

Growing Equity Mortgages

A *growing equity mortgage* (GEM) is a fixed-rate mortgage, but with scheduled increases in monthly payments over time. As the payments increase, the excess money is applied to reduce the principal balance of a loan. It gives borrowers the benefits of the low initial payments possible with thirty-year mortgages, but the lower overall interest costs and faster equity build-up found in twenty- or twenty-five-year mortgages, all without having to refinance periodically. Growing equity mortgages on condos and townhomes are eligible for Federal Housing Administration (FHA) insurance, providing borrowers with good interest rates and low up-front costs. There are some limitations on GEMs if the property is an apartment-to-condo conversion. The conversion must have occurred at least one year earlier. In addition, the borrower must have been a tenant at the time of the conversion, or a majority of the tenants must have voted for the conversion. Finally, at least 80% of the FHA-insured loans in the project must be to owner-occupants.

No-Document Loans

The so-called *no-doc mortgages* are usually more accurately called low-document mortgages. They are usually recommended for people who do not have traditional W-2 tax forms for income verification.

You should be aware that some mortgage brokers will push you into a no-doc loan program with higher down payment requirements and higher interest rates, even though you might qualify for a traditional loan with a little extra work. Tax returns for the last two years, bank statements, or letters from employers might be enough documentation to get the cheaper interest rates.

Still, a wide variety of people might not have the ability, or the desire, to share their financial information with a lender. At one end of the spectrum are people who work for cash and do not report very much of it to the IRS—this is not a recommended practice, but it does happen with a great deal of frequency. The other extreme consists of people with complicated financial lives who support very nice lifestyles, but a wide variety of tax write-offs that result in income tax losses every year. It is a little difficult to fit into the requirements for a conforming loan on a $300,000 condo when you have no W-2s and your tax returns for the last three years seem to indicate you are losing about $250,000 per year. Still other people have substantial assets they simply do not want to disclose to anyone for privacy reasons.

There are three main types of low-doc/no-doc mortgages. The *stated income mortgage* is usually for self-employed people or those who make their living from commissions or tips. A *no-ratio loan* means the borrower cannot fit within the loan-to-income ratios because he or she has a complicated financial life, or the borrower is in a transitional time and between jobs or marriages. This might be appropriate for someone with very little income, but who receives large child support payments each month, or for someone who lives off his or her investments. Finally, the true no-doc is the *NINA* (no income/no asset verification), which is for the most creditworthy people who are not willing to share any financial information at all, but are willing to pay the price tag through higher interest rates.

The Right Loan Arrangement for You

Traditional fixed-rate mortgages tend to be the safest loans for buyers, since the interest rate is locked for the entire term of the mortgage. When mortgage rates are at or near historic lows, it is a good idea to take out a fixed-rate loan.

Adjustable-rate mortgages (ARMs) have lower initial interest rates than fixed-rate alternatives, but the borrower bears the risk of rising interest rates in the future. ARMs are most appropriate when mortgage rates are high, but expected to decline in the future. The lower initial rates on ARMs make it easier to qualify for a loan, since lenders base their loan decision on the size of your initial loan payment.

When shopping for adjustable-rate loans, look for loans that have the longest adjustment interval. Loans with interest rates that adjust every three years are usually better than loans that can be adjusted annually. With some ARMs, you can lock in the rate for up to ten years. Most adjustable loans have interest rate caps that limit the size of the interest rate adjustment. The smaller the interest rate cap, the better. The same goes for the initial interest. The lower the beginning interest rate on the ARM relative to the rates on fixed-rate loans, the better.

ARMs can be particularly attractive for condo buyers who do not expect to be living in their unit for more than ten years or so. If you play your cards right, by the time the interest rate on your ARM catches up to what you would have paid on a fixed-rate loan, you will have probably sold your condo. Even if you decide to stay long-term, it should be possible to refinance when interest rates moderate.

Used wisely, interest-only loans can get you into your condo or townhome sooner and with less strain on your budget, at least in the early years of the loan. If you are planning to live in your unit for the rest of your life, make sure you will be able to handle the higher payments once debt reduction begins. Retirees who do not anticipate significant income increases in the years to come should probably avoid interest-only loans.

Chapter 8:
Different Types of Lenders

Fortunately for you, the American government is solidly in favor of home ownership and does everything in its power to help support and promote it. This favorable environment allows a great number and variety of lenders, and one of the lenders will be perfect for you.

Traditional Sources of Residential Mortgages

It seems like there is a constant bombardment of advertisements by lenders wanting to help with home purchases. Television, radio, Internet, billboards, bumper stickers, signs in bathroom stalls—no advertising medium is without an ad for some kind of lender. The different types of lenders can be broken down into four categories:

1. banking or credit union lenders, who take in deposits and make loans;
2. mortgage bankers, who do not take deposits but who use other ways to raise money in order to make loans;
3. mortgage brokers, who do not take deposits and do not loan any of their own money; and,
4. government programs.

As a general rule, government programs assist the neediest people, who might not have any other options. Mortgage brokers have the widest possible selection of loan programs to fit your particular needs.

Banks and mortgage bankers will have the most flexibility and are more willing to consider non-credit score indications of trustworthiness, including general reputation in the community. This is not to say you should avoid one category in favor of another. Investigate all your options and choose the deal that is best for you.

Specialized Co-op Lenders

Many lenders are scared off by co-op apartment loans because there is no traditional real estate interest on which to take a mortgage—the co-op apartment owner buys stock, which entitles him or her to a lease on a particular unit. Still, there are some specialized co-op lenders. For more information, ask the co-op board for some recommendations, check with your state's banking department, or search the Internet. The following sample of co-op lenders includes New York City lenders, as well as lenders who make loans in other regions.

Apple Bank for Savings
800-333-2775
www.theapplebank.com

CitiBank, FSB
800-374-9700
www.citibank.com

**Bank of New York
Mortgage Company**
800-247-4900
www.bnymortgage.com

**Dime Savings Bank
of Williamsburgh**
800-321-3463
www.dimedirect.com

Bank of America
888-293-0264
www.bankofamerica.com

Emigrant Mortgage Company
800-364-4726
www.emigrant.com

Chase Mortgage
800-873-6577
www.chase.com

HSBC Bank USA
800-622-7759
www.hsbc.com

Washington Mutual Savings
800-788-7000
www.wamu.com

VA Guaranteed Loans

The *Veterans Administration* (VA) will guarantee certain loans made by banks or other lenders to qualified veterans, up to a maximum amount of about $57,000—they do not actually loan the money directly. Most lenders require that the VA guarantee, plus any down payment, equal at least 25% of the value (or purchase price, whichever is less) of the unit. The eligibility rules for length of service are rather complicated, and range from ninety days to six years, depending on the circumstances and timing of your service. Eligibility also depends on whether you served in war time or peace time, as well as whether you served on active duty or National Guard, or held some other status. For more information, contact the Veterans Administration at **www.va.gov** or 800-827-1000.

With a VA guarantee, lenders can approve somewhat riskier loans, at lower interest rates, and with little or no down payment. In addition, borrowers can qualify even if up to 41% of their income is used for debt service. This is higher than typical underwriting requirements for non-VA loans.

The borrower must live in the unit and not use it for rental income, be a satisfactory credit risk (under lenient VA guidelines), and have a stable source of income. In order to obtain the guarantee, the veteran will usually have to pay a 2% fee, and eligible Reserve/National Guard members will have to pay a 2.75% fee. These fees can be reduced by paying a down payment. Any lender or broker can help you with the details.

You will need a *Certificate of Eligibility*. If you do not already have one, it can be obtained from your local VA office by completing VA Form 26-1880, "Request for Determination of Eligibility and Available Loan Guaranty Entitlement." You will also need a VA appraisal, called a *Certificate of Reasonable Value* (CRV). The lender usually orders that. Otherwise, the process is pretty much the same as it is for any other loan, except that you must advise your lender that you want a VA guarantee.

FHA Insured Loans

The *Federal Housing Administration* (FHA) is a part of the Department of Housing and Urban Development (HUD). FHA has a goal of increasing home ownership among low-income and middle-income

Americans. To encourage that, it insures certain loans made by conventional lenders. The FHA does not make any loans itself, but because of the insurance it provides, lenders are able to stretch a bit and loan money to people who might not otherwise qualify. Condos and townhomes are eligible under the Section 234(c) program, and co-op apartment loans are eligible under the Section 203(n) program.

These loans are not limited to borrowers with credit problems or low income, but they do assist those who might otherwise not be able to obtain financing. Qualified borrowers must have been discharged from bankruptcy at least two years earlier, been paying on a Chapter 13 plan for at least twelve months, or had a foreclosure no more recently than three years earlier. All judgments must have been paid in full before closing, but collections accounts do not have to be paid if you have *mitigating factors* (essentially, a legally good excuse). Usually, your credit report must show a history of four or more creditors with good payment records. If you do not have that many, you can use evidence of timely rent payments, utilities, or car insurance. The required down payment is usually only 3%, and the money can be a gift from someone else.

If you still do not qualify because of credit problems, you can add a co-borrower with good credit to the loan—the co-borrower does not have to actually occupy the property with you. There is a limit on closing costs that can be charged to the borrower. The size of an FHA insured loan is limited, though, ranging from a current high of $172,632 in some parts of the country to $362,790 in others. To check your area's limits, visit **https://entp.hud.gov/idapp/html/hicostlook.cfm**.

INSIDER TIP:

Homeowners who lost their property in presidentially-designated federal disaster areas can obtain 100% financing. Disaster victims do not have to buy property in the same area as their lost home—they can relocate, if they want.

Other than eligibility, the basic difference between a VA guaranteed loan and an FHA insured loan is the thing that comes with all insurance—an insurance premium. The VA does not impose an insurance premium, because it is a guarantee program. On the other hand, it does charge a funding fee, so it is not an entirely free program. The FHA does charge a mortgage insurance premium, but you can finance it by combining it into the total loan. The normal FHA mortgage insurance premium is 1.5% of the purchase price, which is paid up front or rolled into the loan. There is also a monthly mortgage insurance premium of 0.5%. The monthly insurance payment drops off completely when you reach certain equity levels—usually 78%.

The FHA has some other, specialized loan programs for particular classes of borrowers. The *Teacher Next Door* program offers up to a 50% discount off the asking price for homes being sold by HUD, for teachers living in the neighborhoods in which they teach. The *Officer Next Door* program offers a similar incentive for law enforcement officers who live in the community where they work.

The Department of Housing and Urban Development comes into ownership of homes when an FHA-insured borrower defaults and the lender has to foreclose. After foreclosure, HUD buys the home from the lender, and then tries to resell it as quickly as possible. For more information, visit **www.hud.gov**, or call the Department of Housing and Urban Development customer service center at 800-767-7468.

> # MYTHBUSTER
> ### Condo purchasers do not have to pay the FHA mortgage insurance premium
>
> This myth persists because it was true at one time, due to complicated and inscrutable reasons having to do with government accounting. For more information about the specifics of insured condo loans, call the toll-free FHA Mortgage Hotline, 800-CALL-FHA, and ask for booklet 365-H(7), "Questions About Condominiums."

USDA Loans

The *United States Department of Agriculture* (USDA) offers direct loans and loan guarantees for people living in rural areas. People frequently think of such loans as being for farms only, but that is not true—condos and townhomes are also eligible.

The *Section 502 Rural Development Direct Loans* offer mortgage money that comes directly from the USDA. They are generally available to low-income borrowers who can obtain 100% financing for up to thirty-eight years. Mortgage payments are based on income. More information is available at **www.rurdev.usda.gov**.

There are other USDA-guaranteed loans available for low- and moderate-income borrowers that also provide 100% financing in qualified rural areas. First-time home buyers must take a home buyers' education course if their credit score is below 660. To find out if you are eligible, visit **http://eligibility.sc.egov.usda.gov**, or call 800-414-1226 and ask for the service center for your part of the country.

HUD Loan Guarantees for Native Americans

The HUD Section 184 loan guarantee program was enacted in 1992, and is designed to make home ownership possible on Indian reservation lands, and in off-reservation Indian or Native Alaskan areas. It is limited to Native Americans. This program is necessary because the U.S. government owns all the land on reservations, in trust, for the Native Americans—making it difficult for potential Native American home buyers to borrow money from a bank.

Under the HUD 184 program, money is made available from traditional lenders, who offer federally-guaranteed loans. Condos and townhomes are eligible. Loans are administered by the Department of Housing and Urban Development. For more information, call 800-561-5913, or visit **www.hud.gov/offices/pih/ih/homeownership/184**.

Fannie Mae, Ginnie Mae, and Freddie Mac

Fannie Mae, Ginnie Mae, and Freddie Mac are not government loan programs for consumers, but they are important programs to take into account when seeking financing. Most mortgage loans are combined into huge packages and then sold to large investors (like pension funds and insurance companies), or they are *securitized* and people can invest in them, much like a mutual fund. In order to encourage investment, and thus make more money available for additional mortgage loans, the U.S. government has established a variety of programs.

The federal government established the Federal National Mortgage Association—commonly called Fannie Mae—in 1938. It made no loans, but was authorized to buy FHA insured loans from lenders. In

1968, President Lyndon Johnson ordered it converted to a private company with private investors, because the conflict in Vietnam was such a burden on the national budget that it could no longer afford Fannie Mae. Today, it still makes no direct loans for home mortgages, but simply buys mortgages on the open market, pools them, and then sells them as *mortgage-backed securities*. Fannie Mae is traded on the New York Stock Exchange.

At the same time that Fannie Mae was privatized, Congress carved out part of its functions, placed them under the control of the Department of Housing and Urban Development, and named the new entity the *Government National Mortgage Association* (GNMA). Ginnie Mae, as it is called, guarantees pools of federally-insured or federally-guaranteed loans. Even if a borrower defaults, the investors will still receive their monthly principal and interest payments in full. Contrary to popular belief, Ginnie Mae does not buy or sell mortgages, and does not issue mortgage-backed securities. There is much disinformation on the Internet on this issue, so be careful when researching and rely only on reputable websites.

Congress chartered the Federal Home Loan Mortgage Corporation (FHLMC)—Freddie Mac for short—in 1970, so that Fannie Mae would not have a monopoly on the mortgage loan secondary market. Its purpose was to buy mortgages from lenders, so the lenders would have additional cash to make more loans. After buying the loans, Freddie Mac issues mortgage-related securities that can be bought on the open market. Freddie Mac is listed on the New York Stock Exchange.

Mortgages from Stock Brokerage Houses

Recently, stock brokerage houses have started loaning money for home mortgages. Usually, there is a high minimum loan amount of at least $100,000. Sometimes, you must have a brokerage account with the house in order to receive the loan. Major players include Charles Schwab and Merrill Lynch. If you have a stockbroker, check with him or her for mortgage loan availability.

Assumable Loans

The popular perception of an *assumable loan* is one that can be taken over by a buyer with no credit check, a minor amount of paperwork, and perhaps a $100 assumption fee. That was true many years ago, until the 20%+ interest rates of the late 70s and early 80s, as well as the savings and loan crisis, forced everybody involved to think twice about allowing anyone to simply take over mortgage loans whenever they wanted. Today, you may be able to find a seller who has a no-questions-asked assumable loan, but it is extremely rare. FHA insured loans and VA guaranteed loans are assumable, but the buyer still has to meet underwriting requirements.

The thing that keeps a loan from being assumable is something called a *due on sale clause*. Almost all mortgage loans contain such a clause. If property is sold, the entire loan balance is due immediately. Many Internet and other gurus have schemes for getting around due on sale clauses, but these *wraparound mortgages* and *all-inclusive trust deeds* rely on no one telling the lender that you are avoiding the due on sale clause. If you cannot tell someone what you are doing, do not do it. All such schemes are just that—schemes. Many people have spent the last twenty-five years closing loopholes that allowed assumption without credit checks or any other sort of lender decision making. For the most part, the only time you are possibly going to find a truly old-fashioned assumable loan is if your seller had private financing from an individual, and that individual had poor legal advice when drafting the loan documents.

Using Retirement Money

You have several ways to use retirement money for the purchase of a first home. The biggest problem is satisfying the IRS—play by the rules and you will be okay, but bend the rules and you are looking at hefty taxes and penalties.

Generally speaking, first-time home buyers can withdraw up to $10,000 from their IRA or Roth IRA accounts, penalty-free, in order to pay qualified home purchase expenses, like down payments. Spouses can withdraw up to $20,000 together. There is a lifetime limit, though. Once you use up your distribution free passes, you cannot put the money back in your account and then use it again in the future. Also, remember that you still have to pay taxes on the money, but not the 10% early-with-drawal penalty. For more information, go to **www.irs.gov**, or call 800-TAX-FORM, and get a copy of Tax Topic 428, "Roth IRA Distributions" and Publication 590, "Individual Retirement Accounts."

Although you cannot distribute money from your 401(k) program penalty-free or tax-free, you may be able to borrow money from it. This will depend on whether your particular plan documents allow it. In order to qualify for such a loan, *all* of the following requirements must be met:

- ◆ the loan must be less then 50% of the vested account, or $50,000, whichever is less;
- ◆ the loan must be repaid within five years (unless it is used to buy your primary residence); and,
- ◆ loan payments must be substantially equal and made at least quarterly.

There are some other technical requirements, such as reductions on the $50,000 limit if you already have outstanding loans from the 401(k). Ask your plan administrator for details.

This is not a recommended source of money unless you have absolutely no other choices. It is true that there is no credit check and the paperwork is easy, but you are taking money out of an investment account that is probably earning a pretty high return. If your problem getting a loan someplace else is bad credit, not bad cash flow, then set up the 401(k) loan so you will be paying a high interest rate. That way, you compensate for the lost earnings from the money you have taken out.

MYTHBUSTER

Only first-time home buyers can use retirement money without any IRS penalties

This is technically true, but in practice the category is much broader than that. The IRS definition of a *first-time home buyer* is someone who has not bought a home in the last two years, or the spouse, parent, children, or assorted other relatives of someone who has not bought a home in the last two years. In other words, your grandmother can withdraw up to $10,000 from her IRA to help you buy a house, as long as you have not bought one in the last two years.

Creative Financing Sources

Sometimes no matter how hard you try, you just will not be able to qualify for an affordable mortgage loan, or you will not be able to raise the down payment. There are still some alternatives for you.

The first is to ask the seller if he or she will hold a *second mortgage* for a limited amount of time. Be careful, though, because some loan programs prohibit you from obtaining second mortgages. The thinking is, the higher monthly payments from a first and a second mortgage create more of a financial burden, and make it more likely that you will default on one or both loans. Be sure to ask your lenders and brokers about this option.

Private mortgage insurance (PMI) is available for people who cannot afford the typical 20% down payment required for a home purchase. A separate company insures your lender, for a portion of your loan, in case you default. If the lender forecloses or you sell the property for less than the mortgage amount, the insurer pays it off, up to the insurer's limits. Insurance premiums are paid by the borrower, and can be pretty stout. Sometimes you pay the premium in full at closing. Other times you pay the annual fee at closing, and then pay an additional amount every month. By law, the lender must notify you when your loan balance reaches 78% of the value of the property, and allow you an opportunity to cancel the insurance. Usually "value" is measured by the purchase price of the property, but if you have experienced significant appreciation, you might want to request termination at 78% of the *current* value rather than 78% of the *purchase price.*

Seller financing can occur when the former owner holds a first mortgage on the unit. It is typically available in only two situations. One is when the seller has a difficult property and cannot get a decent price for it in the conventional manner. He or she will agree to hold the financing, knowing that people with poor credit, who have fewer options, will agree to the price just to get the easy financing. The other time you will commonly see seller financing is when someone has no need for cash, but would enjoy earning income higher than he or she could obtain by investing in bank CDs or money market funds. Because of the due on sale clause previously discussed, seller first-mortgage financing is usually available when the seller has no debt of his or her own on the property.

Such sellers are typically retirees moving to smaller homes or heirs selling their parents' property.

Investment financing is another option. To obtain this, find a credit-worthy tenant who would like to share the unit on a somewhat long-term basis—perhaps under a five-year lease. Obtain from that person a lease commitment for a certain term, at a certain rental rate sufficient to pay the mortgage payments, taxes, insurance, and monthly fees. With that in hand, you can sometimes buy the unit as an investment property, based on the creditworthiness of your tenant. You then share the unit with your tenant, and pay a portion of the "rent" each month. Interest rates will be somewhat higher than typical home loans, but it is a way to buy a desirable property when all other avenues seem closed to you. You will have to declare the rental income, but you will also be able to take depreciation and other expenses. Be aware that this cannot be a sham transaction. If you default, and the lender forecloses, the new purchaser might be entitled to enforce the lease. In addition, you and your tenant will be guilty of bank fraud—a federal crime—if the whole transaction is for appearances' sake only.

A Dangerous Lending Alternative

Finally, there is one very risky option that is not recommended, but that can be readily found on the Internet and through brokerage channels. This is the financing practice known as *bond for title, bond for deed*, or *land sale contract.* They all work the same way—a third party buys the unit you want, and you make monthly payments to that party, usually at extremely high interest rates. You have very limited ability to pay the loan off early if your finances improve to the point where you can obtain conventional financing. At the end of the loan term, if you have made all your payments on time, the third party will give you a deed. If you miss one payment, at any point in the process, the third party can declare a default and you lose everything. You might have no right to cure the default, no ability to redeem, and limited bankruptcy rights. Some "lenders" in this area count on the fact that you will default and they will be able to resell the property to some other person. The practice is so predatory, and has such a statistically high default rate, that many states regulate it heavily. Before pursuing this option, talk to a credit counseling agency in your state, and possibly an attorney.

Loan Comparison

It will be easier to compare loan offers if you can put their important terms into a worksheet and look at them side-by-side. The sample loan comparison worksheet on page 95 shows you what terms of each loan you might want to consider. There is also space for you to start your own comparison. Add any additional terms that might be important to you, such as reputation, as you wish.

As in real life, the answers are all over the chart, and not easily evaluated. Loan 3 looks attractive but encourages you to go deeply in debt with little equity in your property. The initial interest rate is low, but can increase more rapidly than the others and result in the highest final interest rate. Loan 2 has a somewhat higher initial rate than Loan 1, but a smaller lifetime interest cap. On the other hand, all of Loan 2 will be due in ten years. Loan 1 appears to be safer, because of the thirty-year amortization, but it might be irrelevant if you cannot afford the higher payments with the higher interest rate, and will need to sell or refinance anyway. There is no right answer, because it will depend on your particular circumstances and risk tolerance. If you need help deciding among your choices, seek the help of a financial planner or accountant.

Loan Comparison Worksheet

	LENDER 1	LENDER 2	LENDER 3	YOUR LENDER
Estimated pre-qualify amount	$240,000	$267,000	$280,000	
Max loan-to-value ratio allowed	80%	90%	95%	
PMI premium and how paid	0	$1,000—once	$18/month	
Amortization period	30 years	interest only	20 years	
Balloon payment due	none	10 years	none	
Prepayment penalty	no	yes	no	
Beginning ARM interest rate	6.5%	6.78%	6.4%	
Cap period	annual	annual	quarterly	
Index	LIBOR	T-Bill	CMT	
Cap per period	1%	1%	½%	
Lifetime cap amount	7%	4%	7%	
Fixed-rate, if available	7%	7.25%	n/a	
Origination points	none	none	none	
Points and other fees	1%	$983	2%	
Estimate of third party expenses	$1,000	$1,100	$990	
Time to close	2 weeks	10 days	4 days	

Chapter 9:
Deciding on Home Features You Want

Once you have decided how much you can afford to spend on your condo, co-op, or townhome and found a lender who agrees with you, the next step is identifying the one that best meets your needs. This is not as difficult as it sounds. Put together a master list of features, amenities, location, and other such things that are important to you. Absolutely everything goes on the list. Then, rank the features from most important to least important.

If you can afford all of them—wonderful. If not, start trimming items off the bottom of the list until you get to something you can afford.

When making up the master list, people often think of things like whirlpool tub, tennis courts, or a swimming pool. This chapter describes a variety of other things that should be part of your decision-making process.

Location Considerations

The three most important things about real estate are location, location, and location. This is an old chant, but just because it is boring does not mean there is no truth to it—your first consideration should be location. There are many important location considerations including:

- ◆ *distance from important locales*—shopping, dining, cultural activities, education, work, health care, schools, travel hubs, public transportation, recreation, and relatives;

- *traffic control*—the entrance/exit is with or against the commuting traffic flow, nearby traffic lights to slow cars, multiple entrances and exits, and turn lanes at exits out of property;
- *impact of environmental factors*—crime, pollution, possible severe weather damage, political subdivisions, and school systems;
- *proximity*—high-speed Internet, wireless phone service, emergency personnel, pizza delivery, day care, and family recreation;
- *primary direction of the unit*—rising or setting sun in your eyes, southern exposure for plant growing, and extra cost for water views;
- *cost of living in a location*—homeowners insurance, flood insurance, and commuting; and,
- *anticipated changes*—gentrification, industrialization, expansion, and speculation.

Answering the questions that location considerations bring up is not always straightforward. Suppose a condominium project has all the recreational amenities you want, but it is thirty-five miles from your place of work. During rush hour, that thirty-five miles can translate into an hour and a half of driving, each way. You will be driving seventy miles a day, 350 miles a week, 17,500 miles per year. Using the 41¢ per mile auto expense of the IRS as an estimator, that is $7,175 per year in auto expense. All that driving will take 750 hours per year out of your life. When are you going to enjoy the recreational facilities at your condo? Might you be better off with a shorter drive and fewer amenities, and then using the money saved to buy season tickets to sports or cultural activities? These are the sorts of balancing decisions you should make.

Your choice of location can also affect which school your kids will go to. Unfortunately, not all school districts are equal. The better ones tend to be found in townships with higher property taxes. Even if you do not plan on having kids, consider that if you expect to sell your unit at some point, many potential buyers do have children. While it may be true that home prices tend to be higher in locations with good schools, the premium is usually recovered on resale.

Safety is another consideration. What are crime rates like in the areas where you are shopping for your unit? Ask the neighbors, your real estate agent, or the local police. This information can also be found online from the U.S. Census Bureau or in libraries if you live in one of the larger cities or near a university.

Length of Ownership

If you plan to own for a short period of time, it will make a difference regarding which financing options work best for you. Also, you will need to think about whether you can sell in the future and recover your closing and sale expenses or not. A *short-term planning horizon* means you probably cannot afford to take huge risks because you may not be able to ride out any market fluctuations. Most people think just the reverse—they want to buy in an area of speculative frenzy so prices will increase dramatically in the next year or two. Take a good, hard look at your tolerance for risk, and whether you can survive any downturn, before making such a decision.

People wanting to own for the long term need to be much more careful about neighborhood stability, well-designed and well-built projects, wheelchair compatible floorplans that might be important in the future, and excellent third-party management. Running away from problems by selling your home probably will not be an option. Whatever has motivated you to search for a permanent home will probably keep you from moving if you are unhappy.

Use of the Home

It seems a little obvious, but vacation homes will have different criteria than full-time residences. However, there are more use considerations to make. Is your home a refuge—a place to escape from the world into privacy and quiet, with cozy rooms and terrific insulation? Do you entertain often and need an open floor plan and some outdoor space for spillover? If you have a home office, will you be allowed to have a home-based business? Think about your lifestyle and choose a residence that will fit those kinds of needs.

Your Particular Unit Features

This is where you think about all the mundane stuff—number of bed-rooms and bathrooms, central air, and so on. Here are a few things you might not think about, though. How much closet space do you need or want? Is a whirlpool tub an essential, or a dust catcher? Do you want ground floor or upper floor, interior entrance off a hallway or exterior off a balcony, eight-foot ceilings or ten? The list can get quite long, but do not let that stop you. You want to think about absolutely everything that might be important, and then later start paring down to what is reasonable. You might be surprised to discover that you care passionately about ten-foot ceilings and everything else is negotiable. Until you completed this exercise, you probably never stopped to think about it in that manner.

The Development

Consider the details of the particular development you are looking at. For example, when you go home shopping in Houston, the real estate agents ask you if you want a part of town with trees. Trees cost a lot extra, it seems. Other little-known development must haves can include the avail-ability of *single room occupancy* (SRO) units for maid's quarters, sufficient parking for two or three vehicles per unit, and dedicated amenities. Just because there is a baseball diamond at one end of the project, for exam-ple, does not mean it will stay there forever. It might be some temporarily empty land until the next building is built in a year or so.

Area Amenities

Usually, the desire for particular area amenities is related to your age and family status. Senior citizens generally want easy access to good health care providers, low-cost dining for routine meal-taking, convenient transporta-tion for travel, and interesting things for the grandchildren to do when they visit. Families with small children need to think about child care, fast food, and convenience of extracurricular activities. You get the idea. Make a list of all the places you go in an average month, or places you would like to go but are too far away. Of the items on the list, how many do you want located within one mile of home? How about three or five miles?

Utilities and Technology

Many areas still do not have high-speed Internet access. If this is something vitally important to you, think about it now instead of afterwards, when it is too late. Even if there is DSL, cable modem, or fiber-to-the-curb in the area, many older buildings simply are not wired to take advantage of it.

Another utility that can be a deal breaker is natural gas. If you enjoy cooking and must have natural gas to cook on, specify to your agent that you want this.

Develop a Checklist

The best and easiest way to compare condo, co-op, and townhome units is to develop a checklist of features developed from the exercises above. Every time you talk to an agent or owner and every time you visit a property, you should produce a clean copy of your list, ask all the right questions, and make good notes of the answers. To this list you should add asking prices, association fees, common area amenities, and unit owner restrictions.

Start with easy questions. What do you consider necessities? What do you loathe? These are the drop-dead questions. If a particular condo development has the wrong answers to your drop-dead questions, move on to consider the next one. *Never* try to talk yourself out of your drop-dead issues because you love something else—like a really cheap price. Long after you have gotten over the thrill of saving $20,000 or $30,000, you will still be living with the daily three-hour commute from the far suburbs you swore you would never inhabit.

The form on page 102 helps you focus your thoughts. Adapt it for your own likes and dislikes.

Home Features Checklist

	Essential	Okay	Unacceptable
Location*			
Number of bedrooms			
Number of bathrooms			
Square footage			
Brick, wood, steel, glass, etc.*			
Size of development			
Age of building(s)*			
Views			
School system			
Daily commute time			
Proximity to public transportation			
Good shape or fixer-upper			
Distance to fire station/hydrant*			
Amenities: (list particulars)			
Amenities:			
Amenities:			
Fire sprinklers*			
Security/door attendant*			
Cable television available			
High-speed Internet available			
Average age of neighbors			
Price range			

NOTE: *The items with an asterisk (*) also affect your insurance premiums. If you are a first-time home buyer, talk to your insurance agent before shopping.*

Comparing Properties

Before going to a property, invest in a digital camera, which can be bought for as little as $30. If you do not own a computer or color printer, you can find cheap and easy printing available at most drugstores or copy centers. You do not need high-quality photos, but you do want to remember which condos looked like what. They tend to blur together after awhile.

Use your checklist to record information about particular properties, and attach copies of the photos. Once you start shopping, you will find it remarkably easy to lay all the sheets out on a table and easily compare properties to each other.

Take photos of everything, and label them immediately. You will be surprised how quickly properties will start to run together in your mind. Details that did not seem important at the time will become more important later, so your photos will help refresh your memory. When you get down to making an offer on a specific unit, photograph everything inside and outside. You want to document what was there when you signed the contract. An amazing number of people will replace expensive appliances, light fixtures, and even cabinet hardware with cheap versions, and then look you in the eye and swear it wasn't so! Visual documentation will help you in these situations.

Chapter 10:
Real Estate Brokers and Agents

Most people will use the services of traditional or full-service real estate brokers when buying their homes. As a buyer, you are not required to enter into a written employment agreement in order to work with a real estate broker (although sellers must do so). Brokers can be extremely helpful in quickly identifying those properties that are most likely to meet your needs and are within your budget. They can usually arrange to show properties at times that are most convenient for you. Moreover, they can provide you with a great deal of information about neighborhoods and the quality of different school districts. They may even be able to help you line up financing for your unit. (See Chapter 11 for information about buying on your own.)

Real Estate Professionals

Although the terms *broker*, *real estate agent*, and *salesperson* are often used interchangeably, they have very different meanings. Real estate brokers are people or firms that hold real estate *broker licenses*, which allow them to market properties for owners. In order to obtain a real estate broker's license, an individual usually must meet educational and prior work experience requirements, pass testing, and obtain certification by a state real estate board or commission. Individuals who are designated as salespersons hold a *salesperson's license*, which allows them to work for a licensed broker. The broker works for the consumer, and the salesperson works for the broker. In many cases, a salesperson's license is a prerequisite for a broker's license.

A real estate agent is a broker or salesperson who represents another individual in dealings with third parties. Agents have a *fiduciary relationship* with the people they represent—their *clients*. Fiduciaries owe an extremely high degree of loyalty and confidentiality to their clients. In real estate transactions, that means the agent must negotiate the best price and terms for his or her

> ## MYTHBUSTER
> ### *Your real estate agent works for you*
>
> **Shoppers often talk about "my real estate agent" when hunting for a unit. Beware! The person you think is out trying to find the best deal for you could actually be a seller's real estate agent, working to get the highest price for them.**

client. Typically, sellers hire real estate agents, and the seller is the client. Anyone who wants to buy the property is simply a *customer*. Think about the different feelings you would have if an attorney referred to you as his or her client, or if he or she called you a customer. That is an important distinction.

How Agents Are Paid

Any real estate broker representing a seller must have a written contract authorizing the broker to act, and spelling out the compensation. Full-service brokers typically work for a percentage of the sale price—as low as 4% in extremely competitive markets, and as high as 10% for properties that are more difficult to sell. Most will agree to cooperate with other brokers and share the commission if another agent brings a buyer to the closing table. The following example illustrates this relationship.

Example:

You are friends with Greg, who is a real estate salesperson in a large office. You ask him to sell your condo for $200,000, and offer to pay him an 8% commission. Technically, your listing contract must be with the broker Greg works for, not with Greg directly. Legally, only the broker can sign a contract with you, even though you do not actually know the broker. Greg's broker's name is Allison. Allison will receive the commission at the closing table.

Allison has an employment contract with Greg. She agrees to pay him 80% of any commission she earns as a result of his contacts or efforts. This is an unusually high commission split, but Allison does not enjoy finding business and Greg is a go-getter who brings lots of business in the door. If Allison did not agree to pay him so much, some other firm in town would steal him.

Allison puts up some signs and runs a few ads for your condo. One day, Sophie calls with a buyer who is interested in making an offer. Sophie is a real estate salesperson with a different firm. Her broker's name is Emma, who has never seen your condo or heard of you or Greg.

Allison is perfectly happy to split her commission 50/50 with anyone who brings a buyer who purchases the property, but the commission can be shared only with another broker. In this case, that is Emma. Emma has an employment contract with Sophie, who is still new to real estate and learning the ropes. As a result, Emma pays Sophie only 40% of any commissions she earns for the firm.

Sophie's person buys your condo for the full $200,000. The total commission paid is $16,000. Here is how it is split up:
- ◆ Allison, the listing broker, gets one-half of the total, or $8,000
- ◆ Allison pays Greg, who got the listing, 80% of $8,000, or $6,400
- ◆ Allison keeps the balance of the $8,000, or $1,600
- ◆ Emma, the selling broker, gets one-half of the total, or $8,000
- ◆ Emma pays Sophie, who got the buyer, 40% of $8,000, or $3,200
- ◆ Emma keeps the balance of the $8,000, or $4,800.

The percentages can vary widely, but that is pretty much how it works.

There are several reasons why it is important for you to know how commissions are divided among brokers and agents. For one thing, if you personally call a listing agent because of a sign he or she has on a property, he or she will think you are not working with any other real estate agent. That will make the listing agent extremely happy, because he or she will not have to split the commission with another real estate firm. If you go pretty far down the road with that agent in negotiations, and then introduce him or her to someone as your real estate agent, the listing agent will be very unhappy with you and could poison the deal. That is because he or she will have already figured out how to spend the entire commission, and you have now taken half of it away. If you plan to work with a real estate agent, but are just doing some preliminary calls, be sure to tell the listing agent that information. You will be happier in the long run.

On the other hand, if you plan to buy solo, without an agent's assistance, it is still good to know the typical commission structure. Very few agents count on obtaining listings and finding buyers. Usually they specialize in one or the other, so they receive only half of the commission. You can use this knowledge to negotiate a price downwards. In the example above, suppose a buyer called Greg to make on offer on your condo. This buyer might guess the commission is 8%, or $16,000 on a full-price offer. That means you would net $184,000 after the commission is paid. The buyer knows that Greg's firm would normally receive only half of the commission, or $8,000. So, the buyer will offer to pay $192,000 for the condo, which gives you exactly what you wanted to make, and it gives Greg and Allison exactly what they would normally earn, but it saves the buyer $8,000. The buyer's offer would need to be worded in such a way that it is clear that the deal depends on Allison agreeing to amend her contract and accept only a 4% commission in this circumstance. This is a fairly routine practice, but you have to tell the agent up front that your offer will include a reduced commission because of the absence of a split. Otherwise, you have the same problems as described in the prior paragraph—dashed hopes, feelings of anger, and possibly a deal gone wrong for no reason you can figure out.

Sellers' Agents

When looking for a property, it is very important that you know who the broker or agent represents or works for. Who is the client? If a real estate broker is working as an agent for the seller, which is a very common arrangement, that broker must try and get the highest price for the seller. Sellers typically have many agents. One is the person whose name is in the ad in the Sunday supplement—the agent who typically obtained the listing agreement from the seller. However, every other real estate agent in town can act as a *subagent* of the first agent.

The listing agent's company must have a written listing agreement in order to represent a seller. Every other licensed real estate agent in town is allowed to freelance on that particular property. No writing is required. The freelancers work for the listing agent, and the listing agent works for the seller. All of them owe duties of loyalty, good faith, and confidentiality to the seller. All of them are trying to get the highest possible price for the seller's unit, because the seller is their client.

The person driving you all over town to look at two dozen different properties could be acting as the agent for all of those sellers, and not as your agent. You are just a customer, not a client. The critical difference is in the answer to the question, "Whose best interests are you looking out for?" You should always ask real estate professionals first, "Who do you represent, legally?"

If you are being shown properties by an agent of the seller, you must be careful not to reveal any information to the agent that could reduce your bargaining position. For example, assume that the asking price for a condo is $275,000. You inform the broker that you are from southern California and stunned at the low prices in this area. You could easily go as high as the asking price, but intend to offer only $250,000. Beware—that broker, who represents the seller, will advise his or her client to reject your initial offer and hold out for the higher price.

It gets a little confusing sometimes, because agents will say things that make you think they are indeed working for you. This is highly illegal and unethical, but it happens all the time. An agent might say to you, "The seller is asking $275,000, but that is high, in my opinion, and I think she'll take a lot less money." That sounds like someone who is looking out for you, and leaving the seller to fend for him- or herself. As a result, you might be tempted to share more information about yourself than you should. Do not forget—that agent legally represents the seller, and has just breached his or her legal responsibilities of confidentiality to the seller. That agent is not going to be any more sensitive to your confidentiality or concerns.

As a practical matter, sellers' agents will usually push properties on which they have listings, because they will get to keep more of the commission. Any time you feel an unusual amount of pressure to buy a particular unit instead of some other one, you should ask the agent to tell you who has the listing. If the agent's company has the listing, take all recommendations with a healthy grain of salt.

Buyers' Agents

There are also brokers who represent buyers as clients. A buyer agency is created by a written agreement between a broker and a buyer. The *buyer's agent* must represent the best interests of the buyer in dealings with sellers and their agents. This type of real estate brokerage agreement should be used when the buyer needs guidance and assistance in negotiating with sellers to purchase real estate.

Buyers' agents are common in larger cities, but more rare in other areas. It is a scary thing for an agent to take on responsibilities to a buyer. What if the agent recommends a home inspector who gives a good grade to a condo in a building with obvious structural problems? The very unhappy buyer will certainly sue the inspector, but could also sue the agent.

Another common complaint against buyers' agents is the failure to reveal important information about neighborhood changes coming in the near future. Many parts of the country still have no zoning laws, so it is important to keep up with planned construction in the area.

Example:

You have a buyer's agent, and she helps you find a luxury condo in a great area for a bargain price. The seller's agent reveals that the owner has been transferred to Venezuela and must sell the unit immediately. This is all true, but you assume that is the reason for the low price—it's not. The deep discount is because an older building two blocks away is being converted to a light-security jail to alleviate overcrowding. Even though your agent probably did not know, you had a right to expect your agent to know.

The possibility of a lawsuit and a concern about providing full information are just two reasons why it is a little intimidating for agents to become buyers' agents. However, good insurance, a good work ethic, and good information can usually put those fears to rest.

First-time buyers and buyers moving to a new location and unfamiliar with local market conditions would be the most likely to benefit from this type of agency arrangement. If you fit into this category, specify that you want a buyer's agent.

Buyers' agents are usually paid by the seller, even though they work for the buyer. That is, they look to the transaction for compensation. The seller's contract with his or her agent will specify a commission. That agent will typically split the commission with any other agent who brings the buyer, even if the agent is a buyer's agent.

Sometimes, though, the seller's agent is unwilling to split a commission. Other times, your agent may find a property that is not listed with a real estate agent, so the seller has not agreed to pay anyone a commission. How does your agent get paid? This is, after all, how he or she makes a living. The answer to this question might be buried in the fine print of the agency contract.

When employing a buyer broker, make sure you find out how the broker is compensated and whether you could be liable for a commission if the seller of the property you are purchasing will not pay the broker. You will almost certainly be liable, but the question is—how much and under what circumstances? Will it be a percentage, an hourly fee, or a flat fee? What if the closing falls through because you change your mind? You might be willing to forfeit your earnest money, but you might also owe a commission under those circumstances.

Ask a buyer's agent the following questions before you hire him or her. (Also see "Finding a Broker with Condo and Townhome Experience" on page 116.) These questions are relevant in any agency relationship. Write down your answers and have the agent, and his or her broker, if any, sign the answers. Attach them as an exhibit to the broker's form contract you will have to sign.

- ◆ What happens if I am interested in a property on which you have a listing already? How do you resolve your conflict of interest between your client—the seller—and your other client—me?
- ◆ Do you recommend inspectors, appraisers, lenders, and so on? How do you determine that they are the best ones with the most fair price?

- ◆ What happens if a seller's agent will not split a commission, or we find a seller who will not pay a commission? How do you get paid and what amount would that be in this case?
- ◆ In your opinion, before we look at a single property, what sorts of things do you have a duty to warn me about?
- ◆ What if I find a property on my own, without your services? Will I be obligated to pay you, or will you be entitled to half of any commission paid by the seller?

Transaction Brokers

In some cases, the broker is not working as an agent of the seller, but is instead acting as a *transaction broker*. In this case, the broker represents neither party to a sales transaction, but instead is serving as a mediator, trying to get the seller and buyer to accept mutually agreeable terms. In most cases, any information given to a transaction broker in confidence must remain confidential, although in the real world, this rarely works out perfectly. It is still in your best interest not to reveal anything to the broker that could adversely affect your bargaining position.

Transaction brokers are becoming increasingly popular. Traditionally, real estate brokers justified most of their commission because of their knowledge of the real estate market and their access to buyers. Today, the Internet has leveled the playing field. Buyers now have unprecedented quantities of information, as well as a means for buyers and sellers to find each other without the services of a broker.

An experienced real estate agent can still assist buyers and sellers with negotiations because of the broker's specialized training and knowledge about property values. Brokers are not appraisers, but they do receive training in how to price property for sellers. You might be convinced a unit is overpriced because it is $20,000 more than other three-bedroom, two-bath, 1,500-square-foot units you have seen. The broker might be able to tell you that although it seems bizarre, units on the west side of a certain street are perceived as being in a different neighborhood as the ones on the east, and so appreciate in value more rapidly.

Transaction brokers also have a role in assisting a buyer in moving through all the steps necessary to reach the closing table. It can be confusing for a buyer trying to choose among different financing options.

Without knowing the etiquette of how much pressure is okay and how much is unreasonable pushiness, the process can be intimidating to someone trying to make sure appraisals, inspections, termite bonds, and title policies are all completed on time. That is where a transaction broker can be very valuable.

Limited Consensual Dual Agency

A *limited consensual dual agency agreement* is more rare than other types of agreements. With this type of brokerage agreement, the real estate company represents both the buyer and seller in the same real estate transaction. It sounds difficult, because it is. How in the world do you try to get the highest price for the seller, and the lowest price for the buyer, when it is the same condo?

The most common situation occurs in something called *designated dual agency*, when one sales agent in a brokerage firm represents the seller and another sales agent in the same firm represents the buyer. Technically, the broker represents both parties, but the broker's sales agents can agree to behave as if they worked for different brokers. Neither one shares confidential information with the other.

The other time this type of agency happens is when the one broker or one agent agrees to represent both parties from the very beginning. Some real estate licensing boards allow it, and do not consider it an ethical quandary.

When considering signing a dual agency agreement, it is very important that you talk with the broker to determine the types of services that will be provided and what types of information will be shared with other parties to sales transactions. The best way to handle this is probably by making a written list. For example, use a green sheet of paper for the information it is all right to share with the seller, and a red sheet of paper

> **INSIDER TIP:**
>
> Both transaction brokerage and dual agency agreements are best suited for more experienced and knowledgeable buyers who need assistance finding suitable properties and completing the various documents associated with a real estate sale, but who are able to negotiate the terms of sale on their own.

to list the information that should be kept confidential. For your part, if something is not on either piece of paper, do not mention it. If you find you do need to divulge something additional, add it to the green sheet or the red sheet—do not take chances.

Who Does the Agent Work For?

Now that you know the different kinds of real estate agents, you understand why it is so important to find out who the agent represents. Before you ask a single question of a real estate broker or volunteer one piece of information about yourself, you need to ask the broker one very important question. You should say, "I am interested in buying a condo. If I talk to you about buying, who do you represent—the seller or me?"

In almost all states, an agent is supposed to tell you who he or she represents, but it works better in theory than it does in practice. That is why you need to ask this question up front. When you get the answer, make an obvious point of writing down the answer. If the conversation takes place over the phone, say:

> *I talk to so many different people that sometimes it gets confusing, so I'm writing this down. Just to confirm, your name is _____ and you say that you [would/would not] be MY agent if you worked with me to find and buy a condo. Is that right?*

Virtually every state now has *agency disclosure statutes*. These laws require that brokers and their salespeople provide prospective buyers with a disclosure statement informing them who they represent. This disclosure must usually occur before the exchange of any confidential information between the broker and the buyer. The tricky part for real estate salespeople is deciding how quickly they must get the form signed. Confidential information could be revealed in the first three sentences of a phone conversation, but agents usually do not get your signature on the form until they are pretty sure you are serious—however they determine that.

In most states, the brokerage company is also obligated to inform buyers about the different type of agency and non-agency brokerage arrangements that are permitted in their state. If a broker or salesperson does not provide you with a disclosure statement, make sure you ask for one before working with him or her.

You can be very candid with an agent who represents your best interests. An agent who represents the seller should be given very limited information about your personal finances and motivations. If you do not want the seller to know that you must buy a condo this week, at any price, then do not tell the agent. Otherwise, you will see an incredible unwillingness to negotiate the price or terms, because the seller will know you are desperate.

Determining the Type of Broker that is Right for You

For most people, using the services of a real estate professional will be the most efficient and practical way to find a new home. It takes a stunning amount of time to educate yourself about the general background of a market, without even focusing on particular properties. It is virtually impossible to think of every possible question to ask, unless you are forewarned to ask them. For example, although it is rare, you might sometimes need to inquire, "Is some part of the common area in danger of being taken by eminent domain in order to build a superhighway?" Everybody within a ten-mile radius knew it was coming, including all the real estate brokers, but you did not, so you did not think to ask. This is the sort of question most people would not think to ask on their own.

In addition, most people are uncomfortable engaging in negotiations. As a result, they end up paying higher prices because the seller, or the seller's agent, can easily detect that discomfort and take advantage of it.

Deciding on the best type of agent is your most important decision. Certainly, you want someone with experience in your price range, part of town, and type of property. Beyond that, buyers' brokers are best, but carry the possibility of increased expenses you will have to bear. Working with sellers' agents or subagents is most common, but you should restrict any confidential information you give them. You do not have to work with just one seller's agent—you can communicate with several, and allow several to show properties to you. It is only fair, though, to tell each that they do not have your undivided attention. Sophisticated buyers shopping for something in the same general neighborhood where they already live are good candidates for the use of transaction brokers.

Finding a Broker with Condo and Townhome Experience

Real estate agents are not all created equal. This is certainly the case when it comes to particular types of properties and the specific locations where you may be shopping for your condo or townhome. Interview brokers before working with them.

Most buyers have a specific objective in mind when they are looking for a condo or townhome—a winter retreat, weekend getaway, or full-time residence big enough for family and friends to visit, just to name a few objectives. The broker you use needs to be able to help you achieve your housing goals. Find out if the broker has experience with and specific knowledge of the types of properties you are searching for. Brokers specializing in condos and townhomes are usually more knowledgeable about these markets than brokers who list and sell all types of properties. It is also important to determine a broker's access to the market. Is he or she a member of the local multiple listing service?

It is not considered rude to ask real estate salespeople how long they have been marketing condos and townhomes, how many listings they have, and in what price range. Test them on their knowledge of the market—which neighborhoods are hot, what prices are like, and what the condo association fees are for the properties you are visiting. Last, and most important, do you feel comfortable talking to and working with this broker? Some questions you should ask any potential agent include the following.

◆ *How long have you been a real estate agent/broker?* The more experienced agents usually have better knowledge of the market, but the less experienced agent might be willing to work harder.

◆ *Tell me what companies you have worked for since you became licensed. How long have you been with this company?* Poorly performing agents usually bounce around among real estate companies a lot. On the other hand, top performers get recruited away from former employers. If there is a high degree of job turnover, find out why. Answers about "personality differences" or "not being appreciated" should be warning signals.

♦ *Do you have errors and omissions insurance?* Do not be shy about asking to see proof of insurance—it is not considered rude. Even the best people make mistakes sometimes. It is easier for an agent to own up to a mistake if he or she has an insurance company backing him or her up to pay the piper.

♦ *How many condos have you listed or sold within the last three years?* What you want to find out here is depth of condo experience, not just real estate experience.

♦ *On average, how long do condos stay on the market here? What do you think makes a difference between a quick sale and a lengthy listing process?* Shorter listing times mean it is more of a sellers' market. You will have advance warning to do your homework thoroughly and be prepared to make a quick offer, with the fewest possible contingencies, if you like a property. A one-hour delay in a really competitive market could mean you lose the property to another buyer.

♦ *Have you ever sold the same condo more than once—first for the original owner, then for the buyer who sold shortly afterwards? Tell me about that experience, how long the condo was on the market, and what the price difference was.* There is no right answer here, but any response you get might be instructive.

♦ *Do you think we're experiencing a condo price bubble? Why or why not? How can I protect myself?* Of course, the answer is just pure speculation on the part of the agent. It is a good idea to get as many opinions as possible, though.

♦ *Can you rank the condo projects in town for me, in terms of best price to overpriced? Do the same thing for amenities, homeowners associations, and monthly dues. Which projects seem to have the highest turnover in owners? Why is that? Which condo developments have the most renters? Which ones have the most owner-occupants? Which ones appeal to particular groups—families, seniors, singles?* You can probably think of a lot more questions. You want to test the agent's knowledge of the local condo market. An experienced, thoughtful agent will have answers for most of these questions. Inexperienced or indifferent agents will be hesitant, speak in generalities, or perhaps just tell you they do not know. There is nothing pushy or rude about asking a prospective agent to educate you regarding the market before you decide to employ him or her.

Special Considerations for Co-ops

If dealing with a co-op, it is vital that you find someone with specialized co-op experience, rather than a general, all-purpose real estate agent. So many of the underlying concepts of co-ops are different from traditional real estate, and even from condos and townhomes. An agent with little or no co-op experience may have some false assumptions about the seller, the unit, the building, or the transaction. For example, the agent might not think to ask if the price includes a parking place, or if that parking place must be purchased or rented separately. In fact, there might not be any parking places available for purchase—other tenants may already have all of them. Such a question would never occur to a condo agent.

Fortunately, co-ops are found in high concentration in limited parts of the country, such as the Northeast, Florida, and California. As a result, it is relatively easy to find agents with such specialized experience. In other parts of the country, where the concept is much more rare, you might be better off flying solo rather than educating an agent who will receive half the commission based on your efforts.

Chapter 11:
Finding Properties On Your Own

Even if you are working with a real estate broker, you may still want to search for properties on your own, and not rely solely on the agent. There are two reasons for this.

1. You can help your agent work more efficiently and find the right property more quickly if you do some initial research that enables you to describe exactly what you want and do not want in terms of what is already on the market.
2. Agents will not tell you about some properties on the market, even if they are perfect for you.

To explain the first reason, imagine this. You and your spouse have a little contest. You each work with your own agent. The first one to find the perfect condo gets one month of foot rubs from the loser. You tell the agent, "I want a 3-bedroom, 2½-bath unit for around $150,000." Your partner tells his or her agent, "I want a 3-bedroom, 2½-bath, ground-floor unit, with covered parking, tennis courts, a dozen sit-down restaurants within one mile, and a condo owners association that uses a third-party management company. I have $30,000 I can use for a down payment, and I can afford to spend up to $1,100 per month on mortgage payments and association dues." While you are still driving around town, looking at dozens of condos that just do not seem right for some reason, your partner will have found the dream unit, signed a contract, and figured out the best place to put the sofa and enjoy daily foot rubs.

Properties You Won't Hear About From an Agent

Real estate brokers obtain *listing contracts* from owners. The contract gives the broker the right to act as the owner's agent for purposes of advertising the property, going out and looking for buyers, showing the property to interested parties, and acting as an intermediary in negotiations. For the broker's efforts, he or she receives a commission, usually 5%–10% of the sales price. If a different real estate agent brings the buyer, then the two brokers split the commission, usually 50/50.

In hot real estate markets, brokers have to work really hard to obtain listing contracts, because people can usually sell their units without the broker's help. As a result, there is a lot of competition among brokers to obtain listings. Owners will be able to negotiate lower commission percentages—sometimes as low as 4%. In the typical real estate office, the broker retains some percentage of the commission, and the agent gets the rest.

INSIDER TIP:

If you are working with an agent, that agent will not tell you about listings posted by discount brokers, unless the seller has advertised, "All Brokers Protected." That means the seller will pay a small commission to any agent who brings a buyer. Usually, the commission works out to be the same amount as your agent would receive in a commission split situation. It is called the selling side of the transaction. The seller saves money on the listing side because he or she has a discount broker rather than a full-service broker.

If an agent has a listing contract with only a 4% commission, then the agent cannot really afford to share that commission with another real estate company. Some agents will tell the other agents in town, "I don't co-op." In other words, they do not share commissions. If they do not share commissions, no other agent in town is going to tell anyone about those properties.

So, even if you are working with an agent, that agent will not show you any properties listed by a broker who will not split a commission. You will have to find those properties on your own.

To make things more complicated, *discount brokers* list properties on the *multiple listing service* (MLS), but do not provide other services traditionally offered by full-service brokers. In other words, the discount broker charges a nominal fee, just for access to MLS. He or she does not show the unit, qualify prospects, network with other agents, otherwise advertise, act as intermediary, or hold the seller's hand during closing. He or she also does not receive a fee capable of being split with an agent who brings a buyer. There is just not enough money to go around.

Some sellers choose to go it alone, without the services of a real estate broker. They might be motivated by a desire to save the money that would normally go to pay a broker. Others, desiring a rapid sale, will price their property below the market, but at a figure they would receive after payment of a commission. Sometimes it is not even a money issue. The seller owns a condo in a hot market, and does not like strangers trooping through the unit. In order to control the sale process completely, these sellers go without an agent.

For all of these situations, you will need to do a little detective work to find available properties. Fortunately, you have lots of resources available to you.

Working without an Agent

Not everyone needs the services of a licensed real estate professional. Going it alone can make sense in some situations. Because of the growing scope of the Internet, it is very easy to obtain local MLS listings and information about for-sale-by-owner properties.

Especially if you are interested in a *for sale by owner* (FSBO, pronounced "fizz-boe") property, documentation will be very important, because neither you nor the seller will have any forms or pre-written contracts. The terms of sale must be negotiated, and a written sales agreement must be drawn up, taking the form of a valid contract that is legally binding on both parties. There is a lot more on this subject in Chapter 14.

Be very clear in your own mind about the *deal points* you are willing to agree to, so there will be no misunderstandings when you talk to listing agents or sellers. Important deal points are things like price, terms (all cash, seller financing, thirty days for property inspections, etc.), and contingencies, such as "but only if I can sell my house before then." It is critically important that you are very clear about these items so you do not accidentally give someone the wrong impression. You do not want someone claiming they have an enforceable contract with you, when you thought you were just chatting. All states require real estate contracts to be in writing before they are enforceable, but there are a lot of tricky exceptions. In addition, you need to remember that a contract to buy a co-op is a contract to buy stock, not real estate. As a result, there might be different rules regarding whether or not an oral contract can be enforced.

How to Find Properties

You can find available condo or townhome units for sale just about everywhere. Check the following places as a start:

- ◆ classified ads in the local newspaper;
- ◆ online classifieds;
- ◆ real estate supplements in Sunday papers;
- ◆ *Showcase of Homes* or similar magazine-style publications;
- ◆ signs on supermarket bulletin boards;
- ◆ the Internet; and,
- ◆ signs on actual properties.

Classified ads are typically divided into sections according to area of the city or county. Some have separate sections just for condominiums, townhomes, and co-op apartments. You cannot always rely on properties being placed in the right part of the classifieds. To be on the safe side, you will need to check as many different places as possible. Most classified ads will be FSBOs. Real estate brokers almost always save their ads for the Sunday supplement.

Online classifieds usually have free browsing, although some require you to sign up for a user ID and password. Be sure to check out more than just the Web page of your local newspaper, especially if you are searching for vacation properties. Newspapers in the larger cities within 500 miles of a vacation spot will usually contain ads for condos or townhomes in the resort area.

Sunday supplements offer the advantage of photos. Brokers buy full-page or half-page ads in order to display their most promising properties. Even if you do not see what you want, you still might want to call brokers if they have several properties in your price range with some of the amenities you want. It is quite likely that they are hooked into a community of sellers with somewhat similar properties. These brokers might have just what you are looking for. Do not overlook the classified portion of the Sunday supplement.

Magazine-format home sale publications are almost always free to the public. Banks, real estate offices, and grocery stores keep a good supply on hand. Larger cities have more than one publication competing for the real estate brokers' advertising dollars. In all likelihood, you can also find one devoted to FSBOs.

The Internet is a great way to expand your search. However, you probably do not want to start out with computer searches. There is so much information available on the Internet that your search can be overwhelming. Until you know more about exactly what you are looking for and where, it is usually a good idea to start with the home sale magazines, and then move to the Internet.

Many real estate brokers have websites with links to the local MLS databases. The MLS service is something maintained by local real estate associations. Members agree to pay a monthly fee, and to list all of their available properties on the service. Brokers and agents who belong to the service may search by any number of fields for price range, location, and amenities. The free public links are stripped-down versions that do not allow as much flexibility, but they are helpful in refining your preferences.

You can go to **www.realtor.org** and type in a city name in order to learn about properties currently listed by brokers. Descriptions will include a great deal of information about the size and feature of these homes, usually categorized by price range. It is even possible to see photos of these properties, and in some cases, take a virtual tour. There are also a number of FSBO-specific websites. Examples include **www.forsalebyowner.com**, **www.homesbyowner.com**, and **www.homesalez.com**.

Believe it or not, many great properties change hands as a result of someone posting a little sign on the local grocery store's public bulletin board. You have seen them before—something for sale, and then a bunch of pre-cut, tear-off strips at the bottom of the paper, with a phone number on each strip. If you are interested in certain neighborhoods, visit the grocers in those areas.

People preparing to put their homes on the market usually clean them very well and put excess furniture and junk into storage. Posting a "want to buy" sign at a self-storage facility can pay handsome rewards. Also, talk to crews with housekeeping services, carpet cleaning companies, or painters. They usually know of properties going on the market long before anyone else.

Last but not least, driving around is a good way to find properties for sale. It is easier with traditional homes, where people can put signs in their yards, but not impossible with condos. Brand-new projects always have lots of colored flags, huge signs, and invitations to open houses. Take advantage of open houses to help educate yourself before you buy.

Special Considerations for Co-ops

Most of the country's co-op apartments are concentrated in Manhattan, which is a peculiar market. Throughout the rest of the country, real estate professionals usually share information with each other, through the vehicle of the MLS. In New York, on the other hand, brokers are very competitive and very secretive. They do not share information. You have to look at many different databases for available properties. As a result, going solo is much more labor intensive. There are a growing number of online services, such as **www.mlx.com**, that attempt to gather information from all sources and make it available to subscribers.

> **INSIDER TIP:**
>
> Most times, if you make good eye contact, look unembarrassed, and ask a direct question requiring a short answer, the other person will answer it, even if he or she does not want to. If the other person seems to hesitate, do not jump into the silence with a clarification or a reason for why you think the information is important. Simply wait there, silently and expectantly, until he or she coughs up the answer. This works 99% of the time.

Real Estate Agent Etiquette

Remember a few guidelines when talking to real estate agents who have listings on properties. First and foremost, they are not tour guides—this is how they earn their livings. Never ask an agent to show you a property unless there is some realistic possibility you might buy it. If you are just window shopping and getting ideas, go to open houses. The agent is there anyway, and your presence does not increase his or her workload. Be honest when asked, and say you are in the very early stages of trying to figure out what you want. That way, the agent does not spend valuable time following up with you every few days until it is clear you are not seriously interested.

Second, no question is considered nosy, pushy, or inappropriate. You should even ask about the percentage of the commission and the split. The agent might not tell you, but if he or she does, it is a good thing to know when calculating how much your offer should be.

Sources of Information about Recent Sales

All deeds for condos and townhomes must be recorded somewhere public. This varies from state to state (and sometimes from county to county, if there is something called a *Torrens System* of recordation available). Call any mortgage broker or lender and ask where the deeds are recorded for your area. You can go to that place and usually find out the purchase price for any property sold recently. This can be important if you are looking at units in a brand-new development. Most units will be identical in size, finish, and details—differing only in the number of bedrooms and views. If the asking price for two-bedroom, beachfront units is $450,000, but you discover from the recorded deeds that many are being sold for $425,000, then you know how much price flexibility there is.

Sometimes the real estate tax assessor will have this information, rather than the recorder of deeds. Other times, it is treated as confidential, but you can figure it out from the publicly disclosed filing fees on the deed. The formulas change from state to state, so be sure to ask how filing fees are calculated.

Example:

Smith County charges a filing fee of $1 per $1,000 of sale price equity. Smith County also charges a filing fee of $2 per $1,000 of mortgage amount. If the mortgage filing fee is $400, then the mortgage must be $200,000. If the deed filing fee is $100, then the equity must be $100,000. This results in a total purchase price of $300,000.

Typically, co-op sale information is not publicly available, because only stock changes hands, not real estate.

Even if you do not have a real estate agent working with you, you can still hire one on a limited basis. In many markets, you can purchase a *broker price opinion*—the opinion of a licensed real estate broker regarding selling prices for properties similar to your requirements. This is not an appraisal, and usually involves no science or research, but is just a simple "horseback opinion." It is more information than you will have on your own, and is generally very reliable.

The key to working without a real estate agent is to gain as much information as possible. You will make better decisions and you will sound more confident when negotiating. By and large, though, a real estate professional adds far more value to a purchase than you can imagine. Due to their extensive knowledge of the market, real estate agents can save you lots of legwork and countless hours of research time. In addition, real estate agents will share information with each other that they would never tell you. They do not mind another agent telling you that information, but they will never give it to you directly. It is just a professional courtesy.

Chapter 12:
Asking the Right Questions as You Shop

Once you have found three condos that seem to be good for your needs, desires, and budget, start asking questions. If you are shopping in one of those rare markets where minutes count, you must immediately make an offer on one of them. For everybody else, resist the urge to offer first and ask questions later. Have a lot of questions, do a little bit more homework, and see huge dividends.

Most often, you need time to sort through all the information you have received, think about how it fits together, and then come up with a negotiating strategy. All the best negotiators have a plan—they do not just go in there and wing it. This chapter tells you what information to gather, and where to get it from. Chapter 13 helps you develop a plan of attack in order to successfully get what you want, at the price you want.

MYTHBUSTER

Asking questions is a part of the negotiating process

It can be, if you want to soften up the seller by asking uncomfortable questions. Such questions would be things like, "Do you think the drug rehab center they are talking about opening across the street will have any affect on property values?" Usually, though, questions are designed to assist in your education before you begin negotiations, so you know where the hot buttons are.

Getting Information from the Listing Agent

The first thing you should do is ask some preliminary questions of the broker, whether it is one working with you or it is the listing agent. These questions are not considered offensive or out of the ordinary. Their purpose is to weed out any properties that are not appropriate.

Start with your drop-dead questions from Chapter 9. The goal is to quickly and efficiently strike out unsuitable properties. If you detest red brick fourplexes with white columns and green shutters, nothing about such a unit is going overcome your revulsion. Do not waste time looking at these properties.

You should also always ask the listing broker, "What property conditions are you required to disclose to me?" Do this before even visiting the property. This is a really important question because, in most states, agents have to disclose anything about the property that is hazardous or that could materially affect your buying decision.

Some states are more specific with their requirements. South Dakota requires disclosure if there has ever been a methamphetamine lab on the property, because of the residual chemicals that can be harmful. Arizona requires an insurance report covering the prior five years. California has a detailed *Real Estate Transfer Disclosure Statement*, as do many other states.

Disclosure statements are usually not *required* until there has been a written offer or a signed contract, but you can be sure the listing agent has a copy on file already, because he or she needs to know the property defects in order to avoid accidentally saying the wrong thing to a buyer and being guilty of fraud.

Agents usually want to control the timing of when they reveal these things, so it happens after you fall in love with the property and are more forgiving. You want to find out first, before emotions cloud your judgment.

After your preliminary, drop-dead questions have been answered, if you still wish to visit a particular property, ask the following questions before setting up a visit.

> ◆ *What is the street address of the unit?* Write the address at the top of a piece of paper—one sheet per property. All of your notes will go on that one sheet. All the properties will start to run together in your mind before very long, so start off your search by being organized.

◆ *How long has the unit been on the market?* Do not be scared off by properties with lengthy listing histories. The owner might have had an inexperienced broker who overpriced the unit, and then changed to a better broker with a more realistic recommendation for the asking price. Sadly, if a property is on the market for an unusual amount of time, the other brokers in town stop recommending it. Ask more questions if you do not like the answer you receive here—there might or might not be problems with the unit or project.

◆ *What is the asking price?* Be sure to inquire about the *asking price*, not the *sales price*. It is a subtle distinction, but "asking price" sets up the seller for an expectation that he or she might not receive what he or she is asking. "Sales price" allows the seller to be a lot more firm with the price. Ask this question after finding out how long the property has been on the market. If the condo has been for sale for nine months, the agent will feel a need to justify the price at this point. He or she will volunteer much more information than if you did not first ask about how long it has been on the market, such as how much it was listed for before, what similar units are selling for, whether or not there is an appraisal, and so on.

◆ *Will the seller take less money?* Even though it happens often, it is always a little shocking when the seller's real estate agent says, "Yes—make us an offer." Even if the agent says, "No, the price is firm," you must still evaluate whether you believe it or not.

◆ *What are the monthly fees?* Of course, you need to know this information, but it is also a softening up question. It creates some anxiety that you are price sensitive.

◆ *Will the seller hold any financing?* This is another probing question. You might not care one way or the other, but a seller who is willing to be the banker and finance your purchase might be a very motivated seller. That translates to some major flexibility on the asking price or terms.

◆ *Are there any warranties?* Some sellers purchase home warranty policies to protect buyers, which gives them an edge over other sellers in a very competitive, buyer-oriented market. This is an indication of a seller who is less than confident about his or her ability to sell the unit quickly and at the full asking price. If you ask about a warranty and the seller reveals there is none, the seller may become uneasy, worrying that he or she is competing against someone who does provide a warranty. Newly constructed properties always have certain warranties imposed by law. Check with a local attorney for details.

♦ *How old is the development?* You might prefer brand-new, you might want broken-in, or you might not care. The answer could lead to other questions, though. A new project might require you to check out the developer's reputation. A more mature one might need some tough questions about monetary reserves and the potential for upcoming assessments.

♦ *How many square feet are in the unit?* If you learn that homes with the features you desire typically sell for $100 per foot, and you find one for $75 a foot, that is far enough below the market price to be suspicious. Ask more questions. On the other hand, if you find one priced at $125 per foot, be sure to ask if that unit comes with a live-in housekeeper.

♦ *How many bedrooms and bathrooms are there and what are their approximate sizes?* The number of bedrooms is sometimes a little misleading. Some properties will list five bedrooms, but one will really be a tiny study or a converted pantry.

♦ *How many parking places does the condo or co-op have? Are they assigned? Do you have to pay extra to use them? Where is there extra parking?* For those of you used to living in the suburbs, it probably never occurred to you that parking is not always plentiful. The answer to this question alone might prove to be a deal breaker for you. Parking is usually not a problem with a townhome, but you do want to know if there is a garage or carport, and how many vehicles it is designed to shelter.

♦ *What school zones service this unit? Are there any magnet schools nearby?* The quality of the local schools is always going to be a big factor in the resale value of any real estate, unless it is located in an area dominated by people who send their children to private schools. The proximity of a magnet school for the performing arts, or for science and engineering, will prove to be an enduring draw, no matter what the general school system is like in that area.

♦ *Are the school zones changing?* It is very rare for neighborhoods to change school zones, but it does happen. Sometimes schools are closed and the zones are consolidated. More often, new schools are built and old zones are split up.

If, after hearing the answers to these question, you are still interested in the unit, the next step is to schedule a viewing. Ask that the seller be present. Both agents will resist, but be firm—unless you are in a sellers' market.

Talking Directly To Sellers

Real estate agents hate for you to talk to the seller. They are afraid one party or the other is going to say something unwise and damage their bargaining edge. The listing agent, for example, does not want the seller getting chatty and casually mentioning the little old lady murdered in the next unit two months ago. The buying agent does not want you volunteering that you just moved to town, are living in a hotel, and are desperate to find something to buy. However, just because it makes agents nervous does not mean you should not ask for a face-to-face meeting with the owner.

To keep the listing agent from jumping in with answers to your questions, start out with questions he or she cannot possibly answer. These would be things like, "Does the dishwasher have adjustable racks?" or "How often do you shampoo the carpets?" or "What does

> **INSIDER TIP:**
>
> People usually get nervous during long silences in a conversation. They start talking a lot more to fill in the empty spaces, and they start babbling about things they would ordinarily never reveal, because they are spending more brain power thinking about making conversation than they are thinking about preserving their negotiating advantage. This knowledge is an important negotiating tool. Do not be so eager to share all your amusing stories and everything you have in common with the seller. Keep quiet. Let the seller do all the talking. Your goal is to get information—not to make a new friend.

your next-door neighbor do for a living?" You probably want about ten or fifteen of these types of questions, so that everyone gets in the habit of you asking questions that do not seem very important, and the seller—not the agent—answering your questions. Then, move on to the really important stuff.

Ten Questions to Ask Sellers about the Unit

There are ten common questions you should ask each seller. As always, write down the questions and the answers. When you look at several units, some of these answers will start to run together. You will not be able to remember who said what, so recording the details of each conversation is important.

◆ *Why are you selling?* You want to find out how much pressure the seller has, which will translate to how much he or she is willing to lower the price in order to sell the unit and move on with life.

◆ *How long has your home been on the market?* The agent probably already gave you one answer, but the agent might not know he or she is the fourth agent with a listing on the property. (Most listing contracts are for six months, and towards the end of that agreement, the agent is starting to get a little desperate to move the property.)

◆ *Did you get a home inspection report recently?* A seller who is antagonistic to the idea of a home inspection probably has something to hide.

◆ *What repairs have you made in the last year?* This lets you know where problems have been, what has been fixed, and what could continue giving you problems.

◆ *What is the soundproofing like in the walls and ceiling? What kinds of thing can you hear from the neighbors?* People are amazingly honest when presented with direct questions.

◆ *What is the social life like here?* There is no best or worst answer here. You might prefer privacy, or you might prefer a robust, interactive community.

◆ *Can you give me a list of your utility bills for the last twelve months?* If the power or heating bills are unusually high, the unit might have issues with insulation. If the water bills are unusually high, there might be runny toilets or leaky faucets.

* *Are there any plans to add amenities or fix up areas of the project?* Sellers will usually tell you everything that is under consideration. They see that as a positive selling point. You might see it as evidence of repairs left too long before being addressed, or it might be evidence that there is going to be a huge assessment to pay for all the improvements.

> **INSIDER TIP:**
>
> Once you get really serious about a particular project, visit it sometime around 4:00 p.m., when the children are out of school and not yet doing homework. How noisy are the hallways? Come back around 8:00 p.m., when the television sets and stereos are on. Return at 7:30 a.m. to see what morning rush hour seems like as people try to get out of the parking lot. Can you see or hear any problems? (Make sure you have a letter from the seller identifying you, so no one mistakes you for a trespasser.)

* *Are there any plans to do away with amenities?* Believe it or not, one yacht club community was planning on selling off the marina in order to build more housing. That would be an important thing for a boat-owning buyer to know.

* *What do you think about the local schools and government services?* Exuberant praise with lots of details is usually a good sign. Guarded answers and generalized things like "they're okay" may indicate problems. Ask more questions. A response that the police drive through the project every night should cause you to wonder why they do that—is it a high crime area?

Special Questions for Mature Projects

A *mature project* is one that is completely built out and turned over to the condo owners. In other words, the developer is now out of the picture.

Many condominium projects have third-party professional management, and some do not. Find out who collects the dues, pays the bills,
and keeps track of the property and the owners. This is who you want
to talk to. Some questions specific to more mature projects that you
should ask include the following.

- ◆ *What percentage of the units are owner-occupied, and what percentage are rented out?* If you want to live in your unit, you
want a high percentage of owners also occupying their own
units. That way, you will know they have interests and concerns that are probably similar to your own. Owner-landlords
generally take a more disinterested view of maintenance,
repair, and improvement issues, and are concerned primarily
with keeping their expenses low.

- ◆ *What is the average turnover rate among owners?* In other
words, how long do people usually own their units? High
turnover could indicate problems, or it could indicate a speculative feeding frenzy.

- ◆ *Who are the owners who seem to be most conscientious about
maintaining standards?* These owners can also be the chronic
complainers. You may want to interview them. You might
not want to live next door to them.

- ◆ *Have you ever had to get tough with anyone about following the
rules?* A facility that finds frequent reason to enforce its rules
might be oppressively rigid, or it might be very sensitive to
quality of life issues. One that has never had to force compliance might have well-behaved residents—or management
might be lazy. Whatever answer you get, ask the person why
he or she thinks the development has been so lucky or
unlucky regarding the rules.

- ◆ *How old is the roof, swimming pool, HVAC system, and so on?*
You want to evaluate any potentially large expenses coming
up in the future.

- ◆ *Can I have a copy of the current Conditions, Covenants, and
Restrictions (or the Rules), along with the dates when particular rules were passed?* Of course, you want to know what the
rules are and if you can live comfortably under them. You
also want to know about recent rule changes, which are usually

made in response to recent problems. Reading them can be instructive.

- *How much is the project insured for, and how do you decide how much insurance you need?* Buying a unit in a project with inadequate insurance can be disastrous if there is a fire, hurricane, or other disaster.

- *Are you involved in any lawsuits, or have you been threatened with any litigation?* A yes answer requires a lot of follow-up regarding details. Do not accept anyone's evaluation that a lawsuit is frivolous. In particular, you want to know if an insurance company is defending the association or if the association has to pay its own attorneys. The absence of insurance counsel could indicate coverage problems, and it certainly indicates the possibility of a large judgment.

> # MYTHBUSTER
> *Owner-managed associations or buildings always save money for the owners*
>
> Generally speaking, an association with third-party management is going to be operated better than one without. In addition, professional managers should be self-supporting by saving money through getting the best prices for repairs and maintenance, and by making sure everyone pays their dues on time. Self-managed projects almost always rely on the goodwill and stamina of one or two people, who could move away or die—leaving behind no written records. Those same people usually feel uncomfortable dunning their neighbors for unpaid dues. It could all be a recipe for mistakes, sloppiness, or even disaster.

- *How often does the power go out?* Frequent power outages are a sign of a building with inadequate service. It is not going to get any better without a huge assessment.

Special Questions for New Projects

New projects are always exciting, but they carry their own risks. The following questions help you remove fear of the unknown—if all the units are not yet built, you cannot know what is going to happen in the future. In addition, many construction problems do not become apparent until a few years after completion. Brand-new does not always mean perfect. You should ask the developer or the developer's agent these questions.

- ◆ *Have there been any physical or financial audits?* You should be worried about more than leaky roofs and inadequate insulation. Was there an engineering report regarding subsurface support? Has an architect signed off that the project complies with the *Americans with Disabilities Act?* Did an accountant sign his or her name confirming the accuracy of audited financial statements? Every scrap of paper you can see is additional insurance that all has been done properly.

- ◆ *Can you provide me with proof of insurance, including a performance and completion bond?* Make sure the developer has enough insurance. A policy with only $3 million in liability limits will not come close to making you whole if the property has major construction defects. In addition, traditional insurance will not help you if the developer walks away from the project before it is completed. Have a lawyer check out the separate performance and completion bond to make sure there are no loopholes for the insurance company.

- ◆ *Have all the utility assessments been paid?* There are often large fees for tying into utility services. If the developer does not pay them, the association or the individual condo unit owners will have to.

- ◆ *Under what circumstances can you cancel my reservation for a unit?* You want a letter saying that the developer cannot cancel your reservation or raise the price, under any circumstances, if you have paid your deposit. Do not be surprised if you cannot get this letter, because the reservation system is designed to give the developer most of the freedom. Ask, though, so there are no surprises. There are some major lawsuits going on today over developers dramatically increasing prices on units and canceling reservations if the owner does not agree to pay more.

- ◆ *What other projects have you personally done, and where are they?* Ideally, you would like to look at some other projects and talk to the owners in order to check out your developer. Beware a developer who says "we've had no projects before this one." He or she may mean that the particular corporation doing your condo has never done another one. Ask searching questions if the answers you receive do not feel right. The developer may be hiding something.

♦ *How many total units is this project approved or planned for, and how many are presently built or under construction?* There is no right or wrong answer, just information you need. What you view as wonderful green space insulating you from city traffic noises might be next year's project of another twenty-five-story building whose residents will look right into your windows. If the developer says the project is completely built out, ask for a site map so you know what he or she is calling "the project." Almost all jurisdictions require developers to file site plans with the state or local government authorities—that becomes a contract with owners regarding what spaces will remain untouched.

♦ *What is the mixture of sizes and price ranges of units in this project? Do you have any nonresidential uses planned?* This is a tricky area. You might buy a luxury condo in a luxury building and then find out the developer reserved 10% of the space for small, inexpensive units in order to obtain favorable financing terms. This might affect your resale value, depending on local opinions on the subject of mixed-income developments. Further, the ground floor might be planned for high-end retail and a fancy restaurant, or it might be set aside for a charter school with high bus traffic twice a day. You should know as much as the developer regarding the plans for the project.

♦ *How many owners hold multiple units, and how many units do they hold?* Again, depending on your goals, there is no right answer here. A large number of units held by a small number of owners could indicate an intention to hold as rental property, or it could mean there is a speculative boom. If association voting is one-vote-per-unit, then a small number of people could control the entire association. Go into your purchase with your eyes open. Nothing is ever perfect.

Co-op and Condo Conversions

Very few developers build projects with the goal in mind of keeping some portion of the units for rental income—they think in terms of huge chunks of money earned from development fees, construction management fees, and profits on sales. As a result, it would be extremely rare to find a brand-new project in which you have to be concerned about the owner's long-range plans. He or she wants to sell as many units as possible, as quickly as possible, and move on to the next project.

This is not true of apartments converted into condos or co-ops. Sometimes the former apartment building owner will do the conversion, and sometimes the owner sells to a third party who converts. If building ownership remains the same, then that person is used to being a landlord and enjoys the regular income. The owner may have agreed to convert the building to condos or co-ops because he or she needed to raise some extra cash relatively quickly, but did not want to go to lenders for one reason or another. Such owners might not be motivated to sell a majority of the units—and the votes—to other people. In most instances, the *offering documents* describing the conversion will also describe the rights and responsibilities of *holders of unsold shares* in a cooperative, and owners of unsold units in a condo conversion. Some courts have imposed a duty on the former owners to sell all their shares within a reasonable time, thereby fulfilling purchasers' expectations that the building will be a true co-op community. These issues raise an element of uncertainty that should be addressed by asking the right questions.

- ◆ *May I have a copy of the offering documents, or whatever documents you have for potential purchasers that describe your plans for this building and the sale of units?* Legally, the owner is required to give this to you anyway, but timing is everything—you want it earlier rather than later.
- ◆ *Do you have any plans to keep some portion of the units for rental income?* This should be in the offering documents, but you want to find out immediately, without having to read a lot of legalese.
- ◆ *What happens if you do not sell as many units as you would like, for whatever reason?* In this situation, the developer might cancel all reservations and return all earnest money deposits. The developer might think this is all right, but by that point

you will have quit shopping and might be at an extreme disadvantage when your search has to begin again. You need to make intelligent decisions based on reasonable expectations regarding the future.

◆ *Are there any long-term leases or long-term contracts (longer than one year) pertaining to this building or project? What are they, who are they with, and how are they related to the building owner?* In 1980, Congress passed the *Condominium and Cooperative Abuse Relief Act.* It was intended to protect consumers from pre-conversion sweetheart deals that favored the sponsor or former building owner. These would be things like janitorial services contracts for ten years, at twice the rate charged by competitive companies. One provision of the federal law allowed condo associations or co-op boards to cancel such contracts under certain circumstances. Unfortunately, the law was poorly written and filled with loopholes. Rather than rely on federal protections, you should inform yourself about any such contracts and evaluate how they might affect your decisions if allowed to continue into the indefinite future.

Nine Questions about Finances

The best source for information about finances is the organization's treasurer. Reports might be generated by a management company, bookkeeper, or accountant, but they all end up in the treasurer's hands. Obtain the following information from the treasurer.

◆ *What amount of money do you keep in the reserve fund for unexpected repairs?* There are always unexpected repairs, and a reserve fund for surprises prepares for such things. If there are no reserves, then it is unlikely the association will vote for frequent assessments. The repairs just will not get done, or they will be done in an inferior manner.

◆ *What amount of money do you keep in reserve for capital repairs and improvements?* This should be different from the reserve for surprises. Capital expenditures are big-ticket items like replacing a roof or building an exercise facility. Groups develop different philosophies on this subject. Some like to keep dues low and make assessments when needed. Others prefer higher monthly dues in order to build up a reserve and avoid future assessments. Having a reserve fund is generally more financially prudent.

♦ *Are any assessments planned for the next two years?* Large additional expenses in the near future could make or break a deal. In a new project, many of the amenities you desire might be obtainable only through assessments because the developer ran out of money before project completion.

♦ *When was the last assessment, how much was it, what was it for, and is it a continuing assessment?* Probably the most important question out of this group has to do with continuing assessments. For really massive expenses, like rehabbing a golf course or an entire building, no one can afford a single assessment. The total cost might be spread out over several years of assessments.

♦ *Can you give me the budgeted and the actual operating statements for the past three years?* It is always good to find out how an organization spends its money, and how well it is able to do its financial planning. You might also discover additional questions, such as, "I thought the condo association paid for insurance on the buildings and common areas. Why are there not any expenses for insurance premiums?" Instead, you might discover a huge revenue item entitled "Fines and Penalties." Such a find will prompt a lot more questions, because it indicates a very strict co-op board or condo association that fines heavily and often. You never know what you will discover when you take the time to read financial statements.

♦ *May I have a copy of a current aged-payables report?* In other words, you want to find out if all the bills are being paid on time. If they are not, the group has problems that are not going to get any better without some sort of intervention (like firing a bad treasurer) or dues increase.

♦ *How often do the dues increase, and are any increases currently planned?* The cost of living goes up every year. Although it is not popular, dues should increase a little bit every year in order to keep up with increased expenses. An association that keeps dues stable for many years, in the face of increasing expenses, has to cut the quality or amount of services in order to stay within its budget, unless it has some independent source of income. With a co-op, you may have other considerations such as rent control and rent stabilization laws. This is incredibly tricky. If in doubt about the prospect for rent increases, consult an attorney.

◆ *How many units are currently past due on their dues? What is the total amount you have in past due receivables?* Payment problems could indicate unhappiness with management, or owners in financial trouble. Neither one of these is good for you. Do not be bashful—ask for details and ask what is going to be done to fix the situation.

◆ *Are there any fees or expenses imposed when a sale occurs?* You will most often encounter this in a co-op apartment situation, with the imposition of a *flip tax*, which is not really a tax, but a fee assessed by the co-op as a way of raising extra money when units change hands. Fees can be assessed as a certain amount per share of stock, a flat fee per transaction, a percentage of the purchase price, or a percentage of the profit. Flip taxes are usually paid by the seller, as a matter of practice, but this can vary. Condo associations, learning a lesson from their co-op cousins, are now starting to impose transfer fees as well. Whether this is legal or not is a hotly contested issue in the law. For now, it is legal until a court says it is not. Find out about such fees up front, instead of being forced into the courts to contest it afterwards. (See Chapter 19 for more information on flip taxes and transfer fees.)

Meeting the Neighbors

Talk to the neighbors, because they are usually a lot more frank than the seller. Also, neighbors have a great deal of impact on your homeowning experience. It would be nice to get a sneak peak before closing, to find out their political views or quirky habits, for example.

Before talking to the neighbors, ask the seller for permission. It could be extremely embarrassing for the seller if he or she has not yet disclosed selling plans to his or her friends. In such a situation, you still need to talk to the neighbor, but you should be extremely discreet and reveal nothing about the particular unit for sale.

Approach the neighbors on a weekend, maybe around mid-morning or mid-afternoon. Have a card with your name, address, and telephone number—it is okay if the card is hand printed. Using a card makes you much less threatening. Explain that you are looking into making an offer on one of the units, and just have a few questions to make sure it is a compatible environment for you. Ask if the neighbor has a few minutes to help you. An explanation of the reason for your questions makes it seem much less like an interrogation and more like a conversation. Some of the things to ask include the following.

- ◆ *I am trying to find out if there is a strong homeowners association. Do you go to association meetings? Why or why not?* Maybe the association is considered ineffective. Perhaps there are some pretty fierce political battles.

- ◆ *In my experience, there is usually a dedicated group of people who shoulder most association responsibilities. Is there someone like that here?* Someone running the association is not necessarily a bad thing, but you do want to know this ahead of time—and what the residents think about it.

- ◆ *If I buy, I would like to become active in association affairs. What do you wish they would change around here?* This question can be remarkably revealing. You would be surprised how candid people become when they are not selling their own unit.

- ◆ *Are you thinking about selling your unit anytime soon?* If so, maybe he or she will show it to you, and you might even strike a deal with the neighbor. Further, he or she might reveal that many of the neighbors are thinking about selling, and what horrible secret has prompted such a mass exodus.

- ◆ *How much privacy is there in this building?* You asked the seller the same question, but it is always good to get a second opinion.

Health and Safety Issues

These are the questions that almost no one thinks to ask ahead of time, but that can have a huge impact on your life after a sale, and could even cause you to sell quickly and move again. Start by asking the listing agent or seller the following questions. If he or she does not know, ask his or her advice about who might have the information.

- ◆ *What government services protect the facility?* If you are just outside city limits, you might be protected by the county sheriff's department rather than the police department. If this makes a difference to you, you should know it.
- ◆ *Are there any registered sex offenders in the area?* Most states have websites that are searchable by zip code in order to locate registered sex offenders. It may affect your buying decision if there are some living in the building.
- ◆ *What is the distance to emergency health care facilities?* For people approaching retirement age, or with health and disability issues, this could be an important factor.
- ◆ *What is the rate of violent crime or drug related crime in the area?* Local law enforcement should be able to provide you with these statistics.
- ◆ *Does the building have a history of mold or moisture problems, radon contamination, or any other environmental issues?* People with guilty consciences will usually sidestep this question. Beware! As a practical matter, all lenders today require what is called a *Phase I environmental report* on these issues before they will fund a project. On the other hand, a building owner may be doing a condo or co-op conversion because he or she needs money, but is unable to borrow it because of failed environmental tests.

Curb Appeal

What is the appearance of the townhome or condo development, or the co-op building? This is called its *curb appeal*. Are there any obvious signs of damage to the outside structure or does it appear well maintained? How about the grounds and landscaping? Come back again after a rainstorm. Does the project seem to have good systems for disposing of rain water?

MYTHBUSTER

Curb appeal does not matter

Although the reality is that you will quickly forget what the outside of your building looks like, when you are ready to sell, it is the first thing potential buyers will see, and it will heavily impact and prejudice them.

Take a walk around the property and look for loose bricks, missing mortar, and missing shingles. What is the condition and appearance of common areas such as reception areas, the clubhouse, parking facilities, the lobby, the furniture, and the carpeting? Even nonstructural cosmetic damage can suggest lack of maintenance or future owner assessments.

Remember—all of these questions and all this research should help you negotiate effectively. You need to know the good, the bad, and the ugly so you can use it to your advantage. If there are not any blemishes and you have found a super deal that seems perfect, then be prepared to move quickly and push for an immediate contract signing.

Chapter 13:
How to Negotiate Successfully

Some people really like to haggle. They feel great pride in their negotiating skills and love the process more than the outcome. If you are faced with a seller in this category, do not be disheartened. Play the game out, give them a run for their money, and be prepared to act defeated when you finally reach an agreement.

For others, negotiating is distasteful. These are the people who will most likely seek out the assistance of a broker, because they are uncomfortable negotiating face-to-face with the other party. If you are in this category, but without an agent, then conduct everything in writing. You have the advantage of being able to work through your thoughts, with no surprises when the seller says something unexpected.

To some extent, buyers and sellers are adverse parties. They think they have different objectives. For the seller, it is usually to achieve the highest price or sell the unit quickly. Buyers want the lowest price, even when they can easily afford the full asking amount and know it is reasonable. They may suspect there is room to negotiate on price, they may think the market is soft, or they may just love the fight.

The real object of the negotiation is the sale. What both buyers and sellers need to remember is that if an agreement is to be reached, and a closing is to take place, both the owner and the buyer must benefit from the deal. Although they may hate to admit it, they need each other.

NOTE: *If you do your negotiation through written exchanges, write the following disclaimer across the top of all such communications.*

This writing constitutes general negotiations only. It is not intended as a firm offer capable of acceptance. Any contract between the parties will be written up in something formal called a Contract or an Agreement, and will contain signature lines for all parties.

There is nothing worse than tossing out an idea that might work, only to have the seller say, "Agreed!" before you have thought out all the ramifications.

Basic Negotiation Tactics

Negotiating is like playing basketball or toilet-training children—you have to keep the goal in mind, but you also have to stay flexible in order to respond to unforeseen events. You should also remember that there are at least two parties who want something at the end of the negotiations. You cannot just take what you want—the other side must achieve some of its own goals. The most successful negotiators always allow the other side some sort of a victory, even if it is just their dignity and the appearance of a win. Use the following strategies when negotiating.

- ◆ *Remain open and flexible.* If a seller suggests something novel, listen to it and evaluate it before jumping to conclusions. The seller might be able to justify his or her higher sales price. He or she might point out that you can buy cheaper units elsewhere, but you will end up paying much higher association dues, for example.

- ◆ *Always be aware of your options.* This means using all the information you have learned in your market research. If you know that the property is unique, tread more carefully in negotiations. Knowing that you have lots of options makes you more willing to lose this particular deal if the seller will not go along with your offer.

- ◆ *When talking to a seller, be very precise about your facts, and be in control of them.* Think about a firm statement such as, "Comparable units in pre-WWII apartment conversions, located within three miles of major employers, recreational opportunities, and reputable schools, typically bring only $115 per foot, but you are asking $135 per foot." This is a much better statement than, "Gee, your price seems a little bit higher than others I've seen." The more knowledgeable and confident you seem, the better chance you have of getting what you want.

♦ *Never insult the seller.* Insulting the seller will not soften him or her up—it will just make him or her defensive and mad. If you have a contrary point of view on some nonmonetary subject related to the unit, begin your comments with, "I'm new to this, but it seems...."

♦ *Think about the seller's motivation.* The seller's motivation is not always to get the highest price. It might be about a quick sale. It might be a desire to sell the unit to a nice person who will be acceptable to the neighbors, who are the seller's friends. If you can figure out what is important to the seller, you can negotiate more favorably.

♦ *If you have limitations, be candid about them.* There is no point in a seller trying to get $250,000 for his or her condo if you firmly believe it is worth only $225,000 *and* that is the absolute most you can afford. Do not start any conversation with your limitations—the seller may have been willing to go as low as $215,000 until you revealed $225,000 was the most you could afford to pay. In any negotiation, the parties try to figure out how much flexibility the other has—how far they can go before they are in danger of crossing a line and killing the deal. Do not make the seller guess. If you seem to be at an impasse on price, you can afford only $225,000, and it turns out that the seller cannot afford to sell for less than $245,000, there will not be a sale unless one or both of you get creative.

♦ *Beware of sellers who will not put a price on their unit, but instead say they are "soliciting offers."* This is a common mistake among sellers who do not have real estate agents. They are afraid to name a price because they are afraid it will be too low and they will leave some money on the table. Your answer, as a buyer, to such a statement should be, "I never price other people's stuff. You will have to name a price, or I'm just not interested."

♦ *Do not bid against yourself.* If you make an offer that is rejected, do not make a higher offer. Ask the seller to counteroffer. If the seller comes back and tells you he or she wants full asking price and that is that, then you have to decide how badly you want that unit.

♦ *Never show fear.* In other words, you cannot fall in love with the condo, and be so obvious about it, that the seller knows he or she owns you. Be cool. Use your poker face.

Price vs. Terms

One of the major tenets of real estate is that you can negotiate price or terms, but not both. This is not strictly true, but a lot of people believe it, so they put *throwaway items* in their terms in order to force you to negotiate terms and then concede to their price. For example, a seller might say, "The price of this unit is $450,000, but closing must take place in ten days, *and* I must be able to live here rent-free for ninety days after closing, *and* when I move, all the appliances, light fixtures, and custom doors are going with me because I need them in the new house I'm building." Do not be intimidated by this tactic—you can negotiate price and terms quite successfully.

Concentrating on Deal Points

You need to think about all the terms of the deal, not just price. If you pay the seller's asking price, you may be able to negotiate other valuable concessions from the owner. If seller financing is part of the transaction, agreeing to the seller's price might allow you to negotiate a lower interest rate from the seller. The savings realized on the loan could more than offset the higher price.

Other items of contention or negotiation include:
- ♦ how much earnest money will be paid;
- ♦ what personal property remains behind;
- ♦ who pays which closing costs;
- ♦ who chooses the closing attorney;
- ♦ how long the buyer will have for due diligence;
- ♦ what contingencies allow the buyer to cancel;
- ♦ what repairs the seller has to make;
- ♦ who is responsible for getting important documents;
- ♦ the closing date;

- ◆ when the buyer can take possession;
- ◆ what obligations the seller has after closing; and,
- ◆ almost anything else that might be peculiar to the deal.

If you think about the deal points that are important to you ahead of time, and then write them down someplace, you will be sure to cover all of them in negotiations. Nothing erodes your position worse than having to return to the seller with "just one more thing." Each time you do that, the seller will feel justified in extracting another concession from you.

Understanding Offers and Counteroffers

The negotiating process usually begins with an offer from the buyer to the seller. Generally, this will be somewhat less than the asking price, unless you are in an extremely hot market. In those situations, real estate agents recommend you make your offer slightly higher than the asking price, just to preempt someone else's offer. It is usually in writing, because real estate agents are obligated to give all written offers to their clients, but there is usually no such requirement for verbal offers. The seller will do one of three things:

1. accept the offer;
2. make a counteroffer; or,
3. reject your offer.

If the seller accepts the written offer by signing his or her name at the bottom, then it is over—you have the property under contract and will proceed to closing, subject only to routine property and title checks. Whether you paid too much or got a steal is no longer an issue. If you are engaged in verbal negotiations, you do not have a firm, enforceable contract until it is put in writing and everyone signs it. This is a special requirement for real estate contracts. States differ in their rules regarding co-op apartments—some say all contracts to buy stock must be in writing, and others say no writing is required. Remember the earlier warning, though—there are many loopholes in the laws requiring real estate contracts to be in writing. Do not get trapped by a loophole and stuck in an accidental contract. Be sure to make your intentions clear—do you have a deal that simply needs to be *papered* (written contract drawn up), or are you still negotiating?

If the seller makes a counteroffer, you then have to decide whether to accept the seller's counteroffer, reject it outright and move on to other properties, or make your own counteroffer. It is a technicality, but once a seller counteroffers, he or she cannot go back and accept your original offer. Here is how that might come up.

> Seller: "I want $200,000 and no contingencies."
> Buyer: "I offer you $190,000 with a home inspection contingency."
> Seller: "I accept your offer of $190,000, but still no contingencies."
> Buyer: "I'll give up the contingency, but only for a $180,000 price."
> Seller: "This is going downhill. I accept $190,000 and the contingency."

Can the seller accept a previous offer like that? No. You do not have a contract if the seller says, "I accept your offer of $190,000 with a home inspection contingency." Step one was an offer to sell. Step two was a counteroffer, and everything after that is a counteroffer. Any time someone makes a counteroffer, everything before that is now void—never to be revived unless *both* parties specifically agree to it.

Listing agents are required to give written offers to their clients as soon as possible. They are not allowed to simply keep offers in a drawer, waiting on some other potential buyers to make an offer, and then present all of them at once to the seller. Of course, an agent can tell his or her seller not to be hasty about accepting your offer, because another one is expected shortly. You should usually write an expiration date into your offers. Otherwise, sellers might be tempted to hold your offer while they go out and shop for someone willing to pay more.

Negotiating Directly with a Seller

You will have to negotiate directly with sellers if you are interested in FSBOs, because there is no broker acting as a buffer or intermediary. Besides getting answers to the questions detailed in Chapter 12, you are trying to find out some information about the seller that will give you a bargaining edge.

The following questions help you evaluate a seller's sophistication.

- ◆ I guess times are changing for the real estate agents. Do you usually buy and sell on your own?
- ◆ What do you and your husband/wife/partner do for a living?
- ◆ Do you have a written contract form, or do I need to find one?

The following questions assist in finding out how motivated the seller is.

- ◆ How long has the unit been on the market?
- ◆ Why are you selling it?
- ◆ Have you bought a new home?
- ◆ Has the association been talking about any assessments?

The next questions let you find out early if the seller is likely to be talkative and eventually reveal things he or she would probably prefer you not know. If a seller loves to talk, let it happen, because the longer he or she talks, the less cautious he or she becomes. If you like the unit, do not be in a hurry to escape from the seller. Say things like the following.

- ◆ Your condo is beautiful. Tell me what you have done with it since you originally bought it.
- ◆ What are the neighbors like?
- ◆ Do you have any advice for us? We're new at this.

If you receive little more than grunts in answer to the previous questions, then try a few more. This time, you want to find out if the seller will become uncomfortable during long silences. When that happens, sellers usually volunteer more information than they should, just to fill the silences. Just make sure you do not ask a question that can be answered with "yes," "no," or "I don't know." After you ask your question and receive the answer, just nod your head and look expectantly at the seller. Do not say anything. Have an expression on your face that seems to say, "what else?" Let the silence stretch to about eight seconds if necessary. One test question should be enough to find out what you want. You do not want the seller panicky and in a rush to get you out of the unit. You just want to know if you have a strong bargaining tool, should you need to use it to find out something important. Any of the following questions can be used as a test question and should require more from the seller than a simple, quick response.

- ◆ What do you especially like about living here?
- ◆ What was this area like when you moved here?
- ◆ The first time you bought a condo/co-op/townhome, was it what you expected?

Negotiating through an Agent

How much success you will have negotiating through a real estate agent will depend, at least in part, on who the broker represents. It goes without saying that if you are using a buyer's broker, you are both on the same team. With a professional at your side, it should be easier.

Sellers' agents are on the other team. A seller's agent is there because the seller needs help negotiating with you. This agent has a duty to represent the best interests of his or her clients. It is very unlikely that these agents will reveal any information to you that could possibly reduce their seller's bargaining position, but it does happen. It never hurts to ask, "How low will the seller go?"

Most of the time, though, the agent will truly try to act as a buffer between you and the seller. The agent will also be showing this property in its best light, pointing out all the reasons you need to buy the property. Treat this information as you would any commercial.

NOTE: *Always keep in mind that even when brokers are not acting as advocates for either the buyer or seller, they work on commission—the higher the selling price, the more they make.*

Negotiating with the Developer of a New Project

In some markets, developers of pre-construction projects do not negotiate anything, except perhaps some small leeway on pricing. Price is the primary thing you haggle about for a used unit, but for something new and still under construction, you usually expect to be able to specify finishes, colors, door swings, and other such matters of taste and style. For example, you might be willing to pay a higher price for ceramic tile countertops instead of Formica, or you might try to negotiate that change for no additional charge. Just remember that you usually have no choices in a hot market.

The color of the carpet, the location of the light switches, the type of tile in the bathroom—you have no decisions, no choices. It sounds incredibly rigid and decidedly anti-customer, but it is the only way affordable condos can be built.

Affordable is a relative term. You might think that someone buying a $1 million luxury resort condo could afford to pay for any changes he or she wants, and you would be right. However, in order to fit that entire complex within the construction budget, every single subcontractor, supplier, and inspector has to be timed to happen exactly on time. If the granite installer drops your countertop and cracks it, he or she has to cut a new one. That three-day delay will cause delays for other subcontractors. Pretty soon it snowballs, and everyone is off schedule. Being off schedule dramatically increases expenses, and it cannot be allowed.

To understand construction scheduling, think about being the tenth car at a traffic light. The light turns green. Does everyone press the accelerator at once and proceed through the light in an orderly fashion? No. The first one goes, then the second car has a little delay before it goes, and maybe the third car waits until the second car is all the way through the intersection before it even starts. Only five cars get through the light before it changes, even though ten should have made it. That is how it is in construction.

If you understand the developer's point of view and reasoning, you will not waste time arguing about things that simply will not change. Concentrate on something else instead—like the price. For more tame markets, developers will usually give you some leeway on finishes. In addition, the earlier in the construction cycle you are willing to sign a contract, the cheaper the price you will be able to obtain. Just make sure—if you are negotiating with a developer—that you require a third-party, independent escrow agent for holding the earnest money or deposit. It has happened before, and it will happen again—developers get in trouble and go broke, and earnest money disappears. Do not let it happen to you.

Documenting Verbal Negotiations

Usually, negotiations consist of a contract going back and forth, with new things constantly added, deleted, overwritten, and then put back in. It is messy and time-consuming. Many people prefer verbal negotiations on all points, and then a written contract.

You need to document the results of those discussions as they happen, and not just at the end. It serves as a reminder of the things agreed upon and the controversial things. It also provides a road map for writing the formal contract. However, nothing scares a seller more than a letter starting with the words, "This is to confirm our agreement...." It sounds like a lawyer and it feels like a setup. The better practice is to write a letter, or send an email, after each round of negotiations. It should say something like the following.

> *I'm glad we have this opportunity to work through our discussions in person (or by phone). Just so we are all on the same page, this is my understanding of where we are today.... If I have missed anything or misunderstood something, please let me know as soon as possible. Hopefully, we'll be able to reach an agreement sometime in the near future.*

Keep doing this for every round of negotiation until you have an agreement on all deal points. The closing language, "hopefully we'll be able to reach an agreement..." makes it clear there is no binding contract yet. When you have agreed on all points, you are ready to write the formal contract.

Chapter 14:
Writing a Contract

Before you start writing, you should know the difference between an offer and a contract. An *offer* is a statement of what you are willing to do and what you would like the other person to do in return. A contract occurs when the other person agrees with everything you said. Legally, a *contract* is a promise by one person in exchange for a promise by another person. The seller promises to sell for a certain amount on certain conditions. You promise to buy for the same amount and the same conditions. It is a little confusing in real estate because most agents refer to that piece of paper that goes back and forth as a contract. It is not actually a contract—it is just a series of offers and counteroffers.

Earnest Money

Earnest money—the money you pay to show you are serious about the purchase—usually has two functions. To a seller, it has *hostage value* to prevent you from walking away from the deal. To buyers, it is an escape hatch if they have a properly worded con-

MYTHBUSTER

It is not a binding contract until I pay my earnest money

Earnest money is not required to make a binding contract. If you sign a contract, panic, and stop payment on the earnest money check, it is too late. The seller still has the option of suing you for breach of contract. The seller might even be able to obtain a court order forcing you to go through with the purchase—a rare action called *specific performance* that does happen sometimes.

tract saying forfeiture of the earnest money will be their only liability if there is a breach. This is vitally important because people who breach contracts are liable for all reasonably foreseeable damages suffered by the other party. In addition, some states have statutes that make defaulting parties pay the legal fees and expenses of the innocent parties.

There is no rule about how much earnest money to offer. Different markets have different general customs. Ask the real estate agent for advice, or check with some local mortgage lenders or brokers—they will know what is typical. Always remember, you might need to walk away from the deal and forfeit the earnest money. Pick a number you can afford, if it comes to that. You might think it would never happen, but it can and does.

Example:

You find the condo of your dreams in a building you have been watching for two years. The only reason you are able to buy this unit at all is because the seller's hairdresser—who is also your sister—tipped you off that it was going on the market in a few days. You immediately rush over and sign a full price contract with $50,000 earnest money and three weeks to close. The next day, you read in the paper that the vacant lot next door to the condo is scheduled for construction of a water treatment plant. Do you still want to buy the unit or do you want to forfeit $50,000? Those are pretty much your only two choices.

Customs vary from market to market, but the parties must agree on someone to hold the earnest money. Under no circumstances should the buyer or the seller personally hold the money. You may both trust each other completely, and you would trust *yourself*, of course, but it is best not to tempt fate. Let someone else have the cash. You could keep it with the real estate broker for the seller, who is required by law to keep the money in a separate *escrow account*. Other times, the closing agent—an attorney, title company, or escrow company—will hold the earnest money.

Some states require earnest money to be held in an interest-bearing account. Others do not have such a requirement, but you can specify it. Choose this option only if the earnest money is sizeable.

Otherwise, the additional handling fees and expenses may be more than the interest you earn.

How to Personalize Real Estate Forms

There is no such thing as a standard real estate contract. Office supply stores, software vendors, local realtor associations, real estate agents, title companies, developers, and lawyers all have their own versions. There is nothing magic about any one of them—except that they tend to protect the person who wrote them. Title company contracts, for example, have lots of clauses in which everyone agrees they will not sue the title company if anything goes wrong. Forms used by real estate companies usually make it clear that the company is not responsible for any of the buyer's due diligence; it does not know anything about any seller fraud; and, if the buyer backs out of the contract and forfeits his or her earnest money, the real estate agent gets half of it and the seller gets the other half.

You might think the way around all this silliness is to write your own contract from scratch. You would be right, but there is one major problem with this theory. Most sellers have real estate agents, and agents generally only like their own forms, and do not want to read yours. They will tell their clients that your contract is a "buyer's contract" and does not protect the seller, even if it has all the same language but in a different order.

Assuming that you are going to be in a situation that calls for modifying someone else's form real estate contract, you may wonder what the best way to go about making changes is. Most people tell you to mark up the form, but that is bad advice, for the following reasons.

- ◆ Real estate contracts are generally printed in small print and single-spaced on legal size paper with tiny margins and no leftover space at the bottom. How can you possibly mark them up and use more than four words per thought?
- ◆ It is not uncommon for the seller to revise your revisions, cross things out, and then agree to requirements that were formerly objectionable, usually by printing a microscopic "ok" next to them. After two or three trips back and forth between you and the seller, a marked-up contract cannot be deciphered anymore.

◆ When you continue to make changes within a contract, you start focusing on the newer language and ignoring the document as a whole. Things that were not important before might be important now, but if you stop reading the contract as a complete document, you forget about some items.

A better way to make offer changes on the document is to write across the top of the contract form, "Additional Terms Attached." Then, write any changes on a separate piece of paper entitled "Additional Terms." Be sure to double space, leave wide margins, and include signature lines for yourself and the seller. At the top of the first page of additional terms, write the following disclaimer:

These terms were specifically negotiated by the parties. If they seem to contradict something in the form contract, then the Additional Terms will control.

If you have to revise the Additional Terms over the course of negotiations, save the old versions, but print out a clean copy every time you have changes. The reason you want to save the old versions is because it might be important later to reconstruct what the parties were thinking as they went through negotiations. One practice is to put a diagonal red line across the front of each form that has been superceded by another one, and then write the date it was replaced. That way, you will not accidentally mix up the contracts.

Important Clauses You Want in Your Contract

Again, there is nothing magic about a contract—you can write one on the back of a grocery store receipt. One party has to agree to sell, one party has to agree to buy, the thing being sold has to be described with some sort of particularity, and you have to say something about *consideration*, or the price tag for the purchase. The consideration could be a specific sum—$185,000—or it could be "at appraised value." All the other clauses are typically the result of negotiations, local customs, or prior bad experiences that someone is attempting to avoid in the future.

One important clause is the Representations and Warranties clause. A *representation* is a statement of fact, and a *warranty* is a promise that the fact is true. This clause is the place where you spell out all the things the seller told you that were important to you in making your decision, and that might have caused you to make a different decision if you had only known the truth. These can be as general as, "Seller represents that it has no knowledge of any defects in the common elements," to something as precise as, "Seller represents that she has never seen a single cockroach, mouse, or other pest in the building."

The Representations and Warranties are important because some states follow the *caveat emptor* rule, usually characterized as *buyer beware*. In those states, a seller of used property is under no obligation to reveal defects to the buyer unless they are so well hidden that a buyer could never find out by him- or herself. In those states, sellers who know that none of the appliances work and the air conditioning is on its last legs do not have to tell you about it, because you could discover the same things with a reasonably thorough inspection. You buy at your own risk, and cannot sue when you discover all the bad news after closing. On the other hand, if a seller tells you that all the appliances are in perfect working order and the air conditioner is brand-new, but all of that turns out to be false, you *can* sue, because the statements would constitute fraud.

People generally hear what they want to hear, and remember what they want to remember. No seller wants an offhand comment like, "You can buy an extended warranty plan for the appliances, if you want," to be remembered as "The appliances are all still under warranty." In order to avoid such instances of selective memory, contracts generally contain a Representations and Warranties clause that says something along the lines of, "Seller makes no representations or warranties unless they are in writing and attached to this contract." You want to make sure you attach a long list of representations and warranties.

Some states require sellers to make certain written disclosures about the condition of the property. Be sure that all such disclosures are attached to any contract as an exhibit.

Other issues that every single real estate contract must address include the following.

Who is the Seller?

The seller could be a person, a group of people, a partnership, a corporation, a trust, a bankruptcy estate, the IRS, or any number of other legal entities. In some states, even though just one spouse owns property, both spouses have to sign a deed in order for a sale to be effective. With a growing trend towards recognition of domestic partners, they too might have claims against property and be in a position to nullify a sales contract unless both sign.

For artificial legal persons like corporations and partnerships, the seller might have to fulfill different technical requirements before it can enter into an enforceable contract. Put a description after the seller's name so the title company can determine if any further steps are required. Examples of such descriptions might be "John Jones, a single man"; "John Jones, Inc., a New York for-profit corporation"; or, "John Jones, Trustee for the infant child Candice Jones."

By yourself, you probably will not be able to sort out all the specialized legal requirements for each of these sellers. You will probably need title insurance to make sure any transfer instruments are executed properly and no one else will have any potential claims to the unit. Co-op apartments do not usually have title insurance because you are buying stock, not real estate. On the other hand, if you are borrowing money to finance the purchase, the lender's attorney will make sure the sale documents are in the right names, with all the proper approvals. Include the short description of the seller in order to save some time for the title company or closing attorney.

Example:

There is nothing worse than selling your old house on Monday, having a condo closing on Tuesday, and then finding out the closing has to be delayed a few weeks because of a delay in the title transfers. The title company discovered at the last minute that John Jones is really a trustee, and a title company lawyer has to review the trust documents to make sure John is not doing anything illegal. John is not worried—he knows he has the power to sell the condo. The title company is not worried—it knows these things almost always work out okay. However, you are homeless for a few weeks. Everything you own has to be packed up, put in storage, and then moved out again after closing takes place—doubling your expenses and doubling the opportunities for damage.

Who is the Buyer?

You are the buyer. However, if you have a spouse, business partners who will share in an office condo, grown children who are on your bank accounts for estate planning purposes, or any number of situations in which you might want more than one person's name on the deed, then you should seriously think about who you want the exact buyer to be. Deciding on who you list as the buyer could affect what happens if you die before closing, whether someone else can enforce the sales contract, and whether someone else will be on the hook for the purchase price.

What are You Buying?

Most condo contracts describe the property as something similar to: *Unit 38 in Lexington Commons, according to a Declaration of Condominium recorded at Miscellaneous Book 189, Page 312, in the Recorder of Deeds of Jefferson County, Connecticut.*

The problem comes when none of the doors have "38" written above them. They all say things like "15B" or "3 West." Or, maybe a door says "38" but it is really unit "37" on the map, because the original unit "1" was split into two smaller units. A numbering scheme on a condo map does not have to match the mailing addresses of the actual units. In order to avoid misunderstandings, you should describe what you are buying in as many ways as possible.

At a minimum, ask the seller for the legal address (or copy it from his or her deed, if he or she is someone other than the developer), but also include a mailing address. If you still have some anxiety, include a plain language description such as, "…being the first unit to the east of the elevators on the fifth floor." You might think it is absurd, but more than one unlucky person has purchased the wrong condo unit from someone who owned more than one of them.

How Much Will You Pay the Seller?

How much you will pay the seller seems like another easy question. The price is the price, right? Generally, this is not a problem, but it is increasingly common for condos to be held by foreign ownership. If the agreed price is $185,000, is that today's U.S. dollars or U.S. dollars on the day of closing? Suppose you are buying from a citizen of Japan. Between contract signing and closing, the value of the Japanese yen drops, relative to the dollar. In other words, your $185,000 might be worth 190,000 yen on the date of contract signing, but only 150,000 yen on the date of closing. Is the seller entitled to more dollars, in order to gain the benefit of the deal he or she thought he or she was making? There are no clear answers, but you should discuss the possibilities if you have a foreign seller, and agree how these possibilities will be handled.

How Will the Purchase Price be Paid?

The most common way to pay the purchase price is to give the seller cash. You might need to borrow the money, but that has nothing to do with the seller.

Sometimes a seller will agree to finance some or all of the purchase price. In that instance, you should spell out the exact terms of the financing arrangement, including the amount financed, the interest rate, when the interest will change (if at all and by how much), whether payments are interest-only or calculated according to some amortization schedule for a certain number of years, and whether or not there will be a balloon payment due after some period of time. You should also be clear about default terms. Do you default if you fail to make one payment on time, are more than sixty days past due, or fail to give the seller proof of insurance?

How Much Earnest Money Will You Pay, and Who Will Hold it?

Earnest money is the amount you pay to show you are serious about buying. Usually a lawyer, title company, real estate broker, or escrow company holds the earnest money. Under no circumstances should the seller be given custody of the earnest money—it is just too easy for something to go wrong and your money to disappear. The seller's licensed real estate broker can hold the earnest money in his or her escrow account and it should be safe. For tactical reasons, though, it would be better if an independent escrow agent held the money.

You want to make sure that forfeiture of your earnest money is the *worst* thing that can happen if you back out on the deal. To do that, you need the following language:

In the event Buyer shall default in its obligation to purchase the property following satisfaction or waiver of all contingencies referred to herein, Seller shall be entitled only to receive and retain the Deposit as liquidated damages, whereupon this agreement shall be null and void and of no further force or effect.

How will Closing Expenses be Split?

This is entirely a matter of contract, and there is no right or wrong split, although there are usually customary ways that everyone splits expenses. Typically, the seller and the buyer will split the cost of the escrow agent or closing company. Usually, they share the cost of the owner's title insurance policy, but the buyer pays for the lender's coverage. Deed preparation is usually paid by the seller, and mortgage preparation is paid by the buyer. Recording fees are generally paid by the buyer, and transfer taxes are paid by the seller. New York City and New Jersey mansion taxes, on properties over $1 million, are paid by the buyer.

What Kind of Deed Will You Receive?

Not all deeds are created equal. The best kind is called a *general warranty deed*. It gives you the most protections, and is the kind customarily used in condo sales. Be sure to specify in the contract that you want a general warranty deed. If the seller will not agree to give you one, find out why and then make an informed decision about how much risk you want to take that other people might have claims against the property.

Bankruptcy trustees, foreclosing banks, the IRS, and any number of other *accidental owners* typically will not give you a general warranty deed, because they do not know what the former owner might have done, so they are not willing to give you very many warranties. They are only willing to sign a lesser kind of deed that gives you fewer warranties, or maybe even none at all. The kind of deed with the least protection to a buyer is called a *quitclaim deed*.

In What Manner Will You Hold Title for a Condo or Townhome?

This requirement does not really have anything to do with the legalities of the purchase. It saves time for the title company, because it prepares a deed from the language in the real estate contract. You save work for the title company if it does not have to change the deed right before closing, when you, for example, reveal that you and your nephew want to have your names on the deed as tenants in common. Just because someone's name is going to be on a deed does not mean he or she has to sign the real estate contract or be contractually bound to go through with a sale. You could sign the contract all by yourself and specify that your name and your nephew's name will be on the deed as tenants in common. If you default on the purchase contract, there is nothing anyone can do to your nephew, because he never agreed to do anything. On the other hand, if you die before closing, your nephew cannot enforce the contract.

Most husbands and wives take title as *joint tenants with right of survivorship*. When one dies, the other one gets the whole property, without going through probate. You do not have to be married to take advantage of this method of owning real estate, and it is not limited to just two people. If the parties have a falling out or go through a divorce, a judge can split the property between or among the owners. If the IRS files a lien against one person, the IRS can force a sale of all the property and then enforce the lien against just the taxpayer's portion of the sale proceeds. Everybody else gets a check from the sale, but the condo or townhome is gone.

Some states recognize something called *tenancy by the entireties*. Only husbands and wives are allowed to hold property this way. When one dies, the other one gets the property entirely, without going through probate. The difference between this type of ownership and joint tenancy with right of survivorship is that nobody can force the parties to split up the property, or to sell it, if one of them does not want to. In other words, any decisions about the property must be unanimous. Even a judge cannot divide the property in a divorce. The good news is that neither the IRS nor any other creditor can take the property, unless there are claims against all the owners. As a result, this method of ownership is frequently used for asset protection purposes.

With a *tenancy in common*, each person owns a percentage share of the property. The shares do not have to be equal. When one person dies, that person's share goes to his or her heirs, not to the surviving other owner. Judges can force a sale, as can the IRS or other creditors. Frequently, business partners or other people who want to share ownership will take property in this manner. It is also popular with second-marriage couples who have children from prior marriages. Such a deed should have additional language allowing the surviving spouse to live in the property and have the full enjoyment of it until death, even though half is owned by the decedent's heirs.

A *life estate with remainders* is an estate planning tool. Especially in a rapidly escalating real estate market, elderly people might want to use this method of ownership. The title is held by the seniors "for and during their natural lives or the last of them to die." Designated people, such as the children, are named as *remaindermen*. The children have no rights of possession or control while their parents are alive. (This is different from a joint tenancy with right of survivorship, in which everyone has equal rights to the property, from the very first day.) When the parents die, the children get the property, but there are no estate taxes, because the children did not inherit the property. They owned it all along—they just were not allowed to use it.

Whose Name Will be on a Co-op Lease?
Buying shares of stock in a cooperative apartment entitles you to a stock certificate and to a *proprietary lease.* You should discuss the same considerations as people buying real estate with deeds, in the prior section.

When Will Closing Take Place?
The law assumes that closing must take place within a reasonable time, but what seems reasonable to you might be outrageous to a seller or a court considering the issue. Under some circumstances, two years might be a reasonable time for the seller to get around to closing. The best strategy is to not leave these things to chance and the whims of a court. Set a date. You can always agree to extend it to clear up paperwork should you need to later.

What Happens if the Seller Cannot or Will Not Close?
Most contracts say that if the seller refuses to go through with the sale, the buyer can either cancel the contract and obtain a refund of its earnest money, or obtain a court order and force the seller to go to closing. If a contract is silent on the issue, the law gives condo and townhome purchasers the remedy of *specific performance* to force the sale. Co-op contracts, being contracts to purchase stock, do not enjoy some of these

traditional protections given to buyers of real estate. Some courts allow specific performance anyway, and others say it is not allowed. This is a good reason to put something explicit about specific performance in your contract.

Recovery of earnest money, or granting of specific performance for the buyer, are good solutions 99% of the time. Problems occur when you have spent money on inspections, surveys, loan commitments, or any number of other things, and then the seller cannot or will not close. If you are going to spend any money prior to closing, make sure you have a clear, written understanding regarding reimbursement if the seller cannot or will not close. For example, include a contract clause saying the seller will be responsible for reimbursing the buyer for any out-of-pocket expenses if the seller refuses to go forward with closing.

What Happens if the Buyer Cannot or Will Not Close?

Perhaps you found out a few days before closing that the next-door neighbor is a registered sex offender. You think the seller should have disclosed this fact, while the seller thinks you should have asked if it were so important to you. You refuse to proceed with closing. What happens?

Some contracts say the seller can keep your earnest money and you have no further liability for any other damages. If the contract is silent on this point, then a court could force you to go through with the purchase, or it could order you to pay many thousands of dollars in damages. Placing a forfeiture of earnest money into the contract at least lets you know how much it will cost you if you walk away from the purchase. It might be more money than is fair, but you are not gambling that a jury will decide the seller's damages are actually much higher.

In rare situations, you might not pay any earnest money. Do not think that lets you off the hook completely. You still have to spell out what happens if you default and do not go through with the purchase. Do you want to be the one to spell this out, or do you want a jury making the decision? A good solution would be to use the following language.

In the event Buyer shall default in its obligation to purchase the property following satisfaction or waiver of all contingencies referred to herein, Seller shall be entitled only to receive $500 as

liquidated damages, and nothing further, whereupon this agree-
ment shall be null and void and of no further force or effect.

Who Pays Association Dues, Outstanding Assessments, and Upcoming Assessments?

Generally, dues are prorated for the period of ownership. If the dues are paid per month and closing takes place on the 11th, then the seller owned the unit for one-third of the month and you will own it for two-thirds of the month. The dues are split accordingly.

Division of outstanding assessments and planned, upcoming assessments might depend on the circumstances and should be specifically negotiated. Standard contract language makes the seller responsible for prior assessments and the buyer liable for ones not yet imposed, even if they are obviously on the horizon. You probably would not object to the seller paying the ones already imposed. What if the owners' association planned to install a swimming pool in three months, and to assess all owners $1,000 for its construction? The pool would really be for your benefit, not the seller's, so it would be fair for you to pay the assessment. It would be a different situation if the association planned a $1,000 assessment because of cash shortfalls in the bank account caused by replacing the roof six months ago. If the association failed to budget for a new roof, kept the monthly dues low, and then found itself in a cash crunch, should the buyer really have to pay for past mistakes? In that instance, it would not be fair for the buyer to pay the assessment, even though it occurs after closing.

Contingencies

Chapter 15 covers real estate *contingencies*, or things that must happen before you are bound to go through with a purchase. After you read that chapter, you will have a good idea of some specialized clauses that should be in your contract. This little section is included here, though, as a reminder for you. If you are going through this chapter, thinking about what to put in your contract, do not forget Chapter 15.

Objectionable Clauses

If the seller or the seller's agent provides the contract, it may contain some clauses that you absolutely must not agree to—or if you do agree to them, only agree after giving them careful consideration.

Open-Ended Damages Clauses

A clause that makes you liable for unlimited damages if you cancel the contract is one of the scariest ones. You might think it is unimportant—there is no way you would ever refuse to close, because you have the cash in the bank and you love the condo. What could happen to change your mind? Most lawsuits arise because someone, sometime, said, "What could possibly go wrong?" Never agree to open-ended damages clauses.

Further, be aware that this clause may not be as obvious as you think. It might say something similar to, "In the event of breach, the parties may elect between specific performance or damages, but may not secure both." On its face, this language seems to be protecting you against double liability, but it is really exposing you to unlimited damages.

Sellers Remaining in Possession After Closing

You want the seller out of the condo before closing. You should inspect the property one last time before closing and make sure the seller did not leave behind a pile of discards in every room, walls dented by movers, or damaged floors formerly hiding under the rugs. Allowing a seller to remain in possession after the closing also creates another problem that should worry you—how long will the former owner take to move out? If the seller refuses to leave after the closing, you may be forced to hire a lawyer for an eviction proceeding. While that is taking place, you may have no place to stay.

Seller Has Made No Representations or Warranties

Sellers like a clause stating that they have made no representations or warranties because it lets them completely off the hook. You have all the responsibility to conduct inspections and to verify everything they told you. Getting them to budge on this clause may be tough. A better solution is to allow the clause, but to make it the subject of one of your modifications. You might say, "except for things listed in the Additional

Terms and Conditions." Do not be bashful—write down everything the seller or the seller's agent told you about the property.

Binding Arbitration

There are several methods of resolving disputes. Lawsuits are expensive, lengthy, and rarely emotionally satisfying. *Mediation* involves a trained person—the mediator—listening to each side and helping the parties work through to a solution. Mediation is not binding, but it is highly effective. Each side feels they agreed to a solution instead of having one imposed on them. A skilled mediator can advise each side, "If this went to court, this is probably what would happen..." Lawyers are usually guilty of what we in the South call "drinking your own whiskey." It means that the lawyers sometimes start believing the propaganda they tell their clients, about how strong the client's case is and what a crook the other side is, and any jury in the world would see it our way. Mediations bring a more dispassionate view to things.

Binding arbitration is very popular with businesspeople, especially developers. Some individuals put binding arbitration clauses in their contracts because they do not know any better, but it is not recommended.

In arbitration, the parties tell their side of the story to someone who is supposed to be a trained specialist in that particular field. For example, you would expect an arbitrator hearing a case about condo defects to know a lot about condos, construction techniques, and repair costs, but this is not always the case. The arbitrator might be ignorant on such issues. Arbitration laws give the arbitrator a lot of discretion, to issue rulings on disputes with virtually no oversight. Most of the time, the arbitrator's decision cannot be reversed, even if he or she is clearly wrong about the law as it applies to a situation—that is why it is called *binding* arbitration. For that reason, you may well be better off objecting to any arbitration clauses. The better practice would be to agree to mediation, or to a jury-waiver (in which a judge but not a jury hears any disputes). Judges have rules they have to observe and they can be overturned if they are wrong, but arbitrators have no such restrictions.

Miscellaneous Other Matters

If there is any question about special items in a unit, make sure you address them in a contract section called "Personal Property." For example, custom draperies can cost as much as $20,000 for just a few rooms. They do not automatically go with the unit under a deed. The old owner might not be able to use the window coverings in his or her new home, but he or she might take them anyway. If you want the draperies, appliances, special light fixtures, or anything else, be sure to specify those items.

Ask for a list of everyone who has keys to the unit. You will want to change the locks after you buy, but might not get around to it for a week or so. It is good to know who might have access.

Write into the contract anything else you are concerned about. Do not be bashful, but do explain your rationale so you do not seem unreasonable. Sometimes there are other ways to allay people's concerns, besides writing longer and longer contracts.

Chapter 15:
Important Contingency Clauses

A *contingency* is an event or action that depends on another event or action taking place. Real estate contingencies generally take the form of a list of requirements before someone is truly obligated under the contract. Most contracts have buyer's contingencies, but there could be some that allow the seller to refuse to go forward. In general, all contingencies fall into three broad categories:

1. things that might make it impossible to close, such as a buyer who cannot borrow money or a seller who cannot deliver good title because of divorce, tax lien, or any number of other surprises;

2. things that change the attractiveness of the deal, such as the buyer's inspection revealing extensive defects, or the seller or the seller losing a promotion and promised transfer to another city; and,

3. things implied by the law in consumer protection statutes, such as a buyer who can cancel the contract if he or she is called up to active military service and shipped overseas, or a seller in some high-pressure situations (like a pre-foreclosure sale) who is given a certain number of days to change his or her mind without penalty.

All contingencies have certain things in common. They allow a contract cancellation without penalty or with a very minor expense, the protected party thinks they are indispensable, and the other side thinks they are unfair and provide back doors to sneak out of deals in favor of something better. Like them or not, contingencies are the grease that lubricates stressful real estate contract negotiations. Without contingencies, there would be so much friction that the parties might never reach an agreement. With contingencies, all parties are forced to agree on the broad parameters of what is fair under the circumstances without having to wait and let a jury tell them.

In many areas, the competition in the condo market is so fierce that sellers laugh at you if you want to put any contingencies at all in your contract. If you choose to go with a no-contingency contract, at least know what risks you are assuming.

Contingencies that Favor Buyers

The four most common buyers' contingencies are (1) financing; (2) sale of prior home; (3) inspections; and, (4) satisfactory review of legal, financial, and insurance documents. Sometimes you will feel comfortable enough to omit financing and sale of prior home contingencies, but you should never give up inspections or document review unless you feel the market is too hot to give you a choice.

In a sellers' market, the more contingencies you have in your offer, the less likely you are to have a seller accept the offer. In a buyers' market, you could probably have eight pages of contingencies, as long as you hold forth some hope that you might buy the unit. The trick comes with neutral, stable markets, in which you must pick and choose which contingencies are important to you. You also have to be prepared to defend them.

Most preprinted real estate contracts have some of the following contingencies in the body of the contract. Whether you are using a preprinted form or your own tailor-made contract, put all contingencies on separate sheets of paper entitled "Additional Terms and Conditions." These pages should be attached to the main contract, and you should require that all pages be initialed by all parties. A section devoted to contingencies would say something like, "All the following items must be completed to Buyer's satisfaction or Buyer may cancel this contract without penalty or liability, and with a full refund of the earnest money." Savvy sellers will want a time limit, such as two weeks or thirty days, after which you must either cancel the contract or it will *go hard*—meaning the contract is binding after that point, even if something goes wrong with one of your contingencies.

When you explain yourself to a real estate agent, and then rely on him or her to communicate your explanation to the listing agent, who then tells the seller, you risk serious misunderstanding. Instead, any written offer should be accompanied by a cover letter explaining all items in the "Additional Terms and Conditions" attachment. Address the letter directly to the seller, but give it to the real estate agent, if there is one. Your goal is for the letter to make its way into the hands of the seller. That way, you do not have to rely on the agent's comprehension, communication skills, or sales ability in order to get your points across to the seller.

Financing Approval

Fortunately, most buyers act in good faith and truly try to secure financing in order to fulfill their real estate purchase contracts. This is a good thing, because this clause is one of the ones most easily manipulated by unscrupulous people. The typical financing contingency allows the buyer to cancel the contract and recover all earnest money if he or she cannot obtain *acceptable financing.* More tightly-written clauses require the buyer to produce a loan commitment letter within a certain number of days.

The financing contingency also provides a little protection against paying too much for a unit, because most lenders require an appraisal before they will fund. If the appraisal comes back in an amount less than your purchase price, the lender will require you to make a larger down payment. The lender will loan 80% (or whatever ratio previously agreed) of the *appraised value,* not the *purchase price.* You have to make up the difference, and if you cannot, then your financing has fallen through.

Be aware, though, that an appraisal is performed for the lender's benefit, not yours. It is not intended to keep you from paying too much money, so you are not allowed to rely on it. As a practical matter, it will be virtually impossible for appraisers to keep up with home values in a rapidly rising or rapidly falling market. Their appraised value in such circumstances is much more of an estimate and more heavily reliant on your contract price rather than market comparables.

If you are buying in a frenzied market, you do not want to risk losing a deal because a seller does not like the financing contingency. It may seem unlikely to you, but plenty of buyers can indeed afford to pay cash for a unit you want. In a cover letter to accompany your offer, mention your current banking relationships and employment, and your belief that you will not have any trouble securing financing. In addition, explain the financing terms you will be seeking (interest rate, term, amount financed) so the seller can evaluate if you are being reasonable or not. It is good to point out that you have been preapproved for financing, but want the contingency just in case. These things will help the seller feel comfortable about your contingency.

On the other hand, if it is a buyers' market, do not bother explaining. These things are personal, after all, and there is no need to share them with strangers if you do not need to.

Financing Appraisal

The financing appraisal is a different slant on the financing contingency. You may elect to forgo the financing contingency because you know there is no way you will be turned down for a loan. However, consider the possibilities. What if the purchase price is $325,000 and you want 80% financing, but the *financing appraisal* comes in at only $300,000? Your lender will loan you only $240,000—80% of the appraised value, not 80% of the purchase price. If you do not have the extra money for the down payment, this could be a deal breaker. Include a financing appraisal contingency if at all possible, to give yourself a way out of the deal if this happens.

Sale of Prior Home

Most people cannot afford a new home without selling their old one. If your present home is under a sales contract, then it is probably going to close on time. Even if it is not under contract, but it is newly on the market in an area of rapid sales, you can reasonably anticipate that you will sell it quickly. Just in case, though, you still need the *sale of prior home* contingency. This allows you to cancel your purchase contract and receive a refund of your earnest money if your own home closing falls through. Without such a clause, you risk more than the loss of your earnest money.

Technically, the seller could sell his or her home to someone else, quickly but for a lower price, and then sue you for the difference.

The sale of prior home contingency is fairly standard and therefore not likely to raise eyebrows. If you think you might meet resistance, explain where you are in the process of selling your home.

Inspections

Beware of any seller who will not let you condition your purchase on the positive results of a professional inspection (unless the market is smoking hot). Most other times, homeowners understand the anxiety you are suffering, and will agree to an *inspection* contingency if you put a short deadline on it and a floor for repairs. In other words, make it clear that you cannot cancel the contract if the inspector discovers a noisy valve in a toilet. Pick a dollar amount, and specify that the contract is cancelable only if the recommended repairs exceed that amount. Use your own best judgment for how high or low that number should be. In a sellers' market, the number probably should be pretty high. In a buyers' market, it can be extremely low.

If it is a hot market and you are told the seller will not accept any contingencies at all, see if you can *buy* a contingency period. Tell the seller you absolutely must have an inspection report, for your own peace of mind. You understand the seller probably has three other buyers lined up, but they are not going to disappear overnight with properties so hard to find. As a compromise, you would be willing to pay the seller some amount of money for the privilege of having a very short inspection period—perhaps three to five days. No matter what happens, the seller can keep that money, because it was fully earned when he or she allowed you the inspection contingency.

Do not assume that a brand-new development does not need an inspection contingency. In an area and time of rapid condominium growth, developers will race to complete projects so they can start others, or might have several projects under development at the same time. Subcontractors will be in high demand. Normally unemployable second- and third-rate plumbers, electricians, and roofers will be able to secure work. As a result, a professional inspection is just as important as it would be for a forty-year-old project.

Your inspection should not be limited to the individual unit you are buying. Critical shared features, such as elevators, should be checked out or at least have their maintenance reports reviewed. Anything that might result in a large assessment for repairs in the near future should be examined by your inspector. This might be as simple as noticing that the parking lot is riddled with potholes, or as subtle as calculating the total amperage capacity for the project's electrical service and comparing that to currently accepted normal requirements.

Satisfactory Review of Documents and Finances

Some of the following items were recommended earlier in this book as things you should do before making an offer. Sometimes you cannot do everything at such an early stage, so that is why you will see some information repeated here. Even if you decided to forgo these items earlier, you must satisfy yourself before closing that there are no unpleasant surprises.

When you buy a condo, co-op, or townhome, you are entering a community with its own government, rules, association fees, and enforcement and punishment mechanisms. You should know what they are before you buy a unit, because every association's approach to rules and enforcement is different.

The title insurance company should ensure that the condominium or townhome development's formation documents were completed and filed properly. There is usually not any title insurance for a co-op, but there will be a title agent, escrow agent, or some other entity to review documents and confirm they are all legally proper. You want to pay close attention to other things, such as the rules and regulations, also called the CC&Rs (Covenants, Conditions, and Restrictions), and to all the provisions in your co-op proprietary lease. You also want to review the association or board minutes for the past two years in order to learn if any special assessments are coming up or if there are recurring problems.

The annual operating statements or financial statements for the past two years will give you a good idea of the items paid by the association as a whole. It will also alert you to potential problems. For example, if you see recurring bills for attorneys or roof repairs, you know to ask more questions. To that end, you should ask for the general journal, the detailed trial balance, or maybe even the check register for the association. An operating statement might have a line item called *contract labor* that looks innocent enough, but that contains bills for the yard crew, a night watchman, *and* a lawyer handling a multimillion dollar lawsuit against the association. That is why you need the details.

The balance sheet will reveal any mortgages or liens on the co-op building or on the common areas of a townhome development. It will also show you if the association has a healthy bank account to cover large repairs, or if you can expect massive assessments when the parking lot needs to be repaved and the elevators overhauled. A large item in *accounts receivable* means some owners have not paid their dues or assessments, and could pose problems for the other owners. Large *payables* entries probably reveal past-due bills.

If you do not see a line item called *contingent liabilities*, ask if there are any. A contingent liability is something that is not actually due today, and might never be owed, but something could happen to make it *ripen* into a liability. The classic type of contingent liability is a lawsuit asking for damages. The most common type in home ownership situations is a government assessment that is being contested, such as dramatically increased real estate taxes, or a disputed assessment for new utilities or road improvement.

If the project is new or still under developer control, you want to review the *pro forma operating statements* and *balance sheets*. They represent the developer's best estimate of what the project's financial affairs will be in the future.

Finally, make sure the project is adequately insured. More than one eager homeowner has purchased a seaside condo only to discover, after the hurricane, that the association's insurance was inadequate.

Common All-Purpose Back Doors

Congratulations! You have just signed a contract to buy an exclusive beachfront condo for $30,000 less than current market price. You have the cash, you have the financing, and the inspector cannot find anything wrong. Two days before closing, you learn the developer has been indicted for bribing building inspectors so they would approve substandard quality steel in the infrastructure. Of course you did not think to write a contingency to cover that. What you needed was a good general purpose contingency to cover bizarre events.

One might be a *fraud, illegal activity, or material change in risk* contingency that states something like the following.

> *If Buyer discovers any fraud or illegality in connection with the project, or any matter which materially increases the risk of loss during ownership, and in Buyer's good faith opinion such fraud, illegality, or material increase in risk substantially affects the value of the property being purchased, then Buyer may cancel this contract without penalty and receive a full refund of the earnest money.*

This clause lets you cancel right up until seconds before the seller signs the deed and you authorize payment. Once closing takes place, however, the contingency disappears and you cannot undo the deal unless the seller itself was guilty of fraud.

You can also insert a generalized *due diligence* contingency, but these typically have short time limits. An example is as follows.

> *Buyer shall have ten calendar days within which to conduct its due diligence. At the end of that time, Buyer may cancel this contract for any reason, without penalty and with a full refund of its earnest money.*

Nervous sellers may require a slight modification, changing the language to read as follows.

> *At the end of that time, Buyer may cancel this contract for any good faith reason associated with its due diligence, without penalty and with a full refund of its earnest money.*

As a practical matter, it is a little difficult to argue with good faith if you assert that you absolutely and in good faith cannot live in a condo with aquamarine tile in the ladies' locker room. The additional language is worthless in most circumstances, but it does help sellers feel better.

Contingencies the Developer Wants

Developers of projects still under construction like a few contingencies of their own. One popular one says that if the project takes longer than twenty-four months to complete, the developer may cancel the purchase contract. It is intended to balance the scales, because consumers are given the same right of cancellation by virtue of the *Interstate Land Sales Full Disclosure Act*, but only if the developer did not register his or her project under the Act. Most developers do not register, because they are not required to under their particular circumstances.

One other clause favored by developers has to do with assignment of the purchase contract. Many people sign contracts to buy condo units before construction is completed for closing upon completion. They do this as investors—they have no intention of ever living in the unit, but just want to take advantage of the pre-construction price discounts, and hopefully, a rapid increase in prices across the board. What they do not like is having to go through their closing at 10:00 in the morning, paying all the closing expenses as buyers, and then flipping the property for a 2:00 pm closing and paying all the closing expenses as sellers. Such people would prefer to sell their contract to someone else, and let that person go through closing with the developer. It is called an *assignment* of the contract.

Developers prefer to have clauses that limit your ability to assign your contract. The developer may prohibit it entirely, or may require that you obtain its permission first. The developer is not being unreasonable or trying to maliciously double up your closing costs. Builders are just keenly aware of how easy it is to sue people in this country, and it makes them very cautious. Legally, it is very difficult for a third party—someone who bought from the first buyer—to sue the developer, but if you have assigned the contract, that person has a direct legal link to the developer. Believe it or not, many developers do full background checks on purchasers in order to avoid potential problems caused by selling units to litigious people.

Clauses the Seller Wants

If sellers were honest, the contingency they want the most would read something like the following.

Seller may cancel this contract without penalty if someone else wanders along and is willing to pay a lot more money.

That is clearly objectionable, but what are some of the other seller contingencies that might find their way into a contract?

The most common seller contingency is the ability to cancel the contract if something happens to change the seller's reason for putting the unit on the market in the first place. For example, an executive being transferred to another city may sell his or her unit. If the transfer falls through or the executive changes jobs, he or she may want to keep his or her home—that is understandable. Such a contingency might read as follows.

Seller may cancel this contract without penalty at any time up until two weeks before closing if there is a material change in circumstances that makes it impractical for Seller to sell. In such event, earnest money shall be refunded in full to Buyer.

If you encounter such a clause, you want to add the following two important sentences.

(1) Despite the foregoing, Seller may not cancel this contract at any time after receiving notice that Buyer has signed a contract to sell Buyer's own home.
(2) In any event, Seller shall be prohibited from selling or leasing to anyone else within one year of cancellation, or shall be liable to Buyer for damages at least equal to the "profit" received by Seller in such sale or lease.

Another seller contingency is the right to cancel the contract if the unit is substantially destroyed by fire, tornado, or other disaster, because the seller might make more money from the insurance than from you. Suppose you offer a low price because the condo has stained carpet, harvest gold appliances, and cheap paneling. After the hurricane, the insurance company does not dig through the debris to find out these things—it pays off full market value for a comparable, but nice, condo. The seller makes more money from the insurance company than from you.

Sometimes you will see a seller contingency called the *terminal illness* contingency. This is common with elderly sellers. Suppose a couple signs a contract to sell their condo. They plan to travel the world for a year or so, and then buy a unit in an assisted living community. Before closing, one of them is diagnosed with a terminal illness and given less than two months to live. They want to cancel the contract and stay where they are, at least until afterwards. With a terminal illness contingency, this can be done.

Chapter 16:
Preparing for Closing

Your job is not finished when the contract is signed. All those contingencies have to be investigated and cleared so that you are satisfied this is a prudent purchase without any potentially terrible surprises. This process is referred to as *due diligence*.

In addition, you need to arrange for a closing company, order utilities, finalize all your financing details, prepare for the physical move, and move the whole process along.

Assistance from the Real Estate Agent

The division of responsibilities among you, the real estate agent, and the lender or mortgage broker is generally a matter of local customs and personal choice. Some agents shepherd the entire process through all the way to closing. They make sure documents arrive in the right places at the right time, and they advise you regarding choosing a reputable home inspector, termite company, and mortgage broker. As the agent's traditional role—access to information not readily available to the public—has been greatly eroded by the Internet, there is often a greater willingness by agents to provide additional services, such as helping you with your due diligence.

Bear in mind, though, that there is a built-in conflict of interest in such help. Even if the agent is acting as your agent, and legally charged with protecting your best interests, he or she does not get paid if you do not close. In such a situation, even the most ethical agent is going to view the toughest home inspector in town as unreasonable. It might be exactly the right inspector for you as a buyer, but the agent will not recommend that person.

With that said, it is common for the real estate agent to recommend home inspectors, title companies, attorneys, and so on. Resist the urge to take the advice without question. Do not rely totally on the agent for due diligence—make some inquiries of your own about people's qualifications, and then allow the agent to assist you in making sure it all gets done in time for closing.

Choose a Closing Agent

One of your first choices involves selecting a closing agent to:

- ◆ handle collection of all paperwork;
- ◆ ensure contract terms are complied with;
- ◆ satisfy lender requirements before funds disbursement;
- ◆ prepare settlement statement and other forms;
- ◆ obtain all necessary signatures on all documents; and,
- ◆ collect all money and pay out properly.

As a matter of custom, attorneys generally perform closings in the eastern United States, and *title companies* or *escrow agents* handle closings in the western states.

You, as the buyer, have the most interest in making the right selection, although the lender must also be satisfied on this point. Your condo or townhome deed, or your co-op purchase documents and lease, must be prepared correctly. Your lender's documents should be correctly filled in, and the loan closing must take place on time, or you might lose your commitment and be forced into a higher interest rate. Most real estate contracts are silent regarding who has the right to choose the closing agent. If yours does not specify, then you should take charge on this item, with the assistance of the real estate agent, if you are working with one. Whether you or someone else makes the choice, you should not wait until the day before closing to ask who is doing the work.

Select a Title Insurance Company

Title insurance protects you in case there is a defect in the seller's title and the seller does not really own the property as a result of some technicality or even outright fraud. Be sure to specify that you want owners and lenders policies—many title companies write only lenders policies unless given instructions otherwise. In the case of a $200,000 condo with a $160,000 mortgage, a lender's policy will cover title defects up to $160,000, and you are out in the cold on your equity. The additional premium to cover another $40,000 worth of risk is relatively minimal.

Many times, the closing attorney or escrow agent writes title insurance for just one company, although there are many different title insurance companies. You may insist that one company do the closing and another provide the title insurance, but why would you get more lawyers involved in a transaction than you have to? As a general rule, every additional party added to the closing will add about 50% to the time involved to get anything done—and with lawyers, time is money.

You can sometimes save money on title insurance premiums by shopping for rates among different companies. If you find out what company insured title for your seller, and can get a copy of the policy, then sometimes you will receive a *reissue credit*, or a discount. Some title companies will give the reissue credit only if they wrote the first policy. Others (more rarely) will give the credit no matter who wrote the first policy.

Deliver Information to the Closing Agent

The closing attorney or title company will need a copy of the sales contract and the name of your lender, if any. It will help speed the process if you also advise them, in writing, of the following matters:

- the full legal name of the seller and spouse, if any;
- any other names by which they are known;
- your full legal name and your spouse's name, if any;
- any other names by which you and your spouse are known;
- the Social Security numbers of all the parties (the seller can give this information privately to the closing attorney);
- the name, account number, and contact information of the seller's lender, if any;

- ◆ the names, account numbers, and contact information for anyone who will be paid out of closing money, including the seller's additional lienholders, because the title company will need to obtain written proof of payoff amounts;
- ◆ any of your prior addresses for the last five years;
- ◆ copies of any powers of attorney that people will be using at closing;
- ◆ whether the seller or the seller's spouse has a guardian or is deceased;
- ◆ whether there are any pending bankruptcy cases in which the seller might be involved (additional approvals may be required before closing can take place); and,
- ◆ the name and contact information for your home inspector, termite company, appraiser, and so on.

The number one reason for closing delays is because the title insurance company has run into a problem and needs extra time to clear it up. Perhaps your name is Josephine Jones and the insurance company has discovered a $500,000 judgment against somebody named "Jo Jones." If the insurance company has your Social Security number and prior addresses, it can resolve the case of mistaken identity fairly quickly. A seller who is a widow or widower might cause some extra work for the title company, because the title company might need a copy of the death certificate or an order from the probate court, so that information must also be disclosed as soon as possible.

Finalize Loan Details

If you have not already done so, you must lock in your lending. Your contract probably has a financing contingency saying it is cancelable if you do not secure acceptable financing. Smart sellers put a time limit on this. For example, the contract might say something like the following.

Buyer shall have fifteen days within which to deliver a loan commitment letter to Seller, or, in the alternative, to remove the financing contingency and proceed to closing.

This means that if you do not have a loan commitment by Day 15, you must notify the seller that the contract has failed and you want a refund of your earnest money, or you must notify the seller that you are no longer relying on the financing contingency and will definitely close on time.

Why do you need to notify the seller even if you do not want to cancel closing? Every single real estate contract is a little bit different, even if it is a form. Tiny changes in wording can have huge consequences. In the example in the prior paragraph, a good argument can be made that if no notice at all is given to the seller, the seller is entitled to believe the contract has been cancelled or even breached. After all, the contract required you to deliver a commitment letter *or* a proceed-to-closing letter. You did neither. In a really hot condo market, you could lose your property, and perhaps your earnest money, on a little technicality like that.

Read the Closing Checklist

Every lender and every closing company has a different set of peculiarities regarding what they require before closing can take place. For example, one lender requires proof of storm sewer service. The only proof necessary is a photograph of a storm drain—which could be anyone's storm drain, in any city in the country—and the lender will be happy. Find out early if there will be any surprises. Aside from that, the checklist will be *your* checklist to shepherd the process through and make sure everything happens on time.

Order Inspections

Usually, a real estate agent will recommend an inspector, but take this advice with a grain of salt. After all, the agent does not want anything happening to prevent closing. You will want to find someone with several years' experience in condos, townhomes, or co-op apartments, and not just detached housing. You want someone who is familiar with all the additional things that require scrutiny, such as the common elements of the development. Ask about professional designations and degrees, and a few examples of inspections that failed. You need a sense of how tough the inspector is. Ask for proof of liability insurance, and do not employ the inspector if he or she acts offended. Be sure to inquire about the need for other, specialized inspectors, such as termite, moisture, roof, or structural engineers.

If the development is new, pay a little extra money and ask the inspector to give you a list of everything that is not yet built. If, according to the offering documents, the project is supposed to have tennis courts and pool, but does not, you need to know that. Even if you do not care about these amenities, you are going to end up paying for them if the builder does not. You need to know what you are getting into.

Termite and moisture inspectors have to be hired. Some termite companies still issue what is called a *repair and re-treat bond*. If termites are discovered after the bond is in place, those companies will pay to repair all damage and will eliminate the termites. Most companies issue only a re-treat bond—meaning repairs are your problem. Virtually every company excludes Formosa Termites from their coverage. These are exceptionally fertile and ravenously hungry termites brought into this country via our southern ship ports, and they are working their way northward. Make sure any inspection separately addresses the issue of toxic mold and any other issues a moisture inspection reveals.

Obtain Important Letters

Reliance letters give you useful information you need, but they also provide information in writing in case there is a dispute in the future. Generally speaking, a reliance letter covers something that is so important you do not want to depend on people's memories about what their answers were.

In addition, you do not want a carefully crafted answer that is absolutely truthful, but is phrased in such a manner that it sidesteps some important information. If you meet with any resistance in obtaining these letters, ask the person why this is an issue for them. Alarm bells should start going off in your head if it is anything other than simple bureaucratic rules that require written permission from someone else (such as the seller) in order to divulge the requested information.

- ◆ If the project is new or still under development, you want something from the construction lender saying the developer is not currently in default, nor has it been in material default within the past year. You must ask the developer for this letter—the lender cannot give it to you unless the developer agrees. It will be from the developer's lender, addressed to you, but the developer will request it for you. There is nothing worse than buying a condo and then finding out the lender has started foreclosure and plans to dump unsold units on the market at half-price.

♦ You should obtain an *estoppel letter* (pronounced "eh-stop-pull") from the association stating that the seller is current on his or her dues and assessments, no assessments are planned or under consideration for the coming year unless disclosed within the letter, and the seller's unit is currently in compliance with all association rules and regulations. *Estoppel* translates loosely to "even if your statement was an innocent mistake, you cannot assert something different in the future if it will cost me more money or make things more burdensome for me." The letter should also officially give you a copy of all rules, regulations, covenants, restrictions, and financial statements for the association, as well as a statement of the current monthly dues and any anticipated changes.

♦ The seller's agent (if there is one) or your agent should give you an *estimated settlement sheet,* showing you the anticipated purchase price, required down payment, closing costs and expenses, and required escrows that will have to be funded at closing.

♦ If school districts, voting districts, or other such things are important factors in your choice of location, then obtain letters from the proper authorities saying the project is within their district and there are no current plans or discussions to change the district lines. Many parents buy condos and then discover their children will be going to different schools next year.

Review Documents

Even if you did this at an earlier stage, review all documents again before closing. Read the association Bylaws thoroughly, all the Conditions,

Covenants, and Restrictions, and the Rules. The paperwork establishing the condominium project, townhome association, or cooperative apartment will also need to be read for things like future plans on vacant land. For new developments, you will need to read the offering documents or prospectus to make sure everything is as rosy as represented. For co-ops, you will need to read your proprietary lease. Also, read all the financial documents for the past two years and all minutes of meetings for the same time period.

This is a tremendous amount of paperwork that could have land mines you will never recognize. It is strongly recommended that you obtain the services of an attorney and possibly an accountant to assist you with this work. Start out by writing down all your beliefs and expectations about the property and the project. The review will be twofold—make sure you are getting all the benefits you think you should and find any land mines. For example, your college town game day condo might prohibit your children from living there while they attend school. A seniors-only co-op might prohibit live-in caregivers. The financials might show pending litigation and no insurance coverage. There is just no way to alert you to all the potential problems—someone experienced in this area needs to read the documents.

Secure Proof of Association or Co-op Building Insurance

Someone will need to obtain proof of adequate insurance by the association for coverage of the common elements and liability insurance. Generally speaking, the title company or closing attorney will order that information from the association if a lender is involved, but not always. If there is no lender, you will have to specify that you want this. You can help prevent last-minute delays and unfortunate surprises, though, if you obtain it yourself and then give it to the title company. No one wants a purchase postponed because the title company went over their checklist the afternoon before closing and discovered they were missing several critical documents. In addition, it is not uncommon to get down to the last minute and discover the association's insurance policy has been cancelled because someone forgot to pay the premium.

Order Homeowners Insurance

Obtain from your insurance agent a *commitment letter* for insurance coverage, and a firm quote of the cost. If your insurance company happens to know that a project is uninsurable because of hidden defects, or premiums will be really high because of constant lawsuits at the project, it would be a good thing if you knew that also—before you go to closing.

Condo and townhome owners will need homeowners insurance with adequate liability coverage. Co-op owners will require specialized co-op insurance. You might want to think about buying a liability umbrella policy that extends your liability coverage up to several million dollars. Usually it is very cheap, compared to the coverage you are receiving.

Most reputable, A-rated insurance companies include a package of endorsements that provide replacement cost coverage for the dwelling and your contents. Be sure to ask about this point, so you are not surprised later to find out you have only fair market value coverage, which is not very much for used furniture, appliances, clothing, and so on.

Mention to your agent any special items that might need to be scheduled separately. You will have to pay a small additional premium for this coverage, but it is worth it. Most policies cover jewelry, for example, only up to a maximum of $1,000 and only if there is a theft. If a hurricane destroys your home and sends your $15,000 engagement ring to goodness knows where, you will wish you had the additional coverage.

Also ask about any specialty endorsements for things such as toxic mold, and other matters that might be excluded from the typical package. Most homeowner policies exclude mold from their coverage, unless you ask for it and pay an additional premium. That endorsement will pay to destroy toxic mold, but you must separately make sure your liability policy also provides coverage, because if you sell your unit and the buyer claims toxic mold problems, the buyer could sue you for health problems he or she claims were caused by your mold. There may be only a slight risk of toxic mold in your area, but it is a trendy new litigation field. You may be at higher risk of being sued for toxic mold than actually having toxic mold.

Assist the Appraisal Process

Usually, the lender orders an appraisal of the property. Your job is to make sure it actually gets completed on time. You will need to find out the name and contact information for the appraiser. The *appraiser* is a trained professional who has access to far more sources of information than you. He or she is also human and subject to mistakes, occasional sloppiness, and frequent computer glitches. Do not for a minute think that just because the appraiser says it, it must be true. Help yourself out by supplying to your appraiser the information regarding any recent sales you think are comparable to your purchase, especially if they are more than your purchase price. A comparable sale would be one that:

- took place within the last year;
- took place in a similar building (e.g., multistory, fourplex, garden home condos);
- took place in a similar neighborhood (e.g., beachfront, urban, upscale, modest);
- had similar amenities (e.g., swimming pool, tennis courts, covered parking);
- had a similar number of rooms (e.g., two bedrooms, two bathrooms); and,
- had similar finishes (hardwood floors, gourmet kitchen, ten-foot ceilings).

Do not worry too much if you cannot find anything very similar to your situation. Just be sure to make a note of which things about the other sales are different from yours. Supply all this information to the appraiser, in writing. He or she will make the appropriate adjustments.

Your job is to make sure that the appraisal is finished several days before the closing is scheduled and before it is given to the lender. Sometimes the appraiser will tell you his or her opinion of value, and sometimes he or she will not—but it never hurts to ask. If the number comes in too low, the lender may require you to bring more cash to the closing table. Since that is always uncomfortable, and sometimes a deal breaker, you want time to persuade the appraiser his or her number is inaccurate because of other factors or information he or she might not have considered. Once that report goes off to the lender, the appraiser will not change it.

Check with Local Governments

Make sure the school districts are where they should be, there are no plans to condemn the property for a highway expansion or a new fire department, and all the health and safety inspections are up to date. Generally, the local government legal department can tell you about any anticipated condemnation proceedings, or direct you to other agencies. The inspections department, where builders go to get building permits, will advise you regarding any periodic inspections they require. Elevators typically must display their most recent inspection in the elevator cab itself. If your contract gives you the right to cancel if you are not satisfied on any of these issues, then you will have to do your homework to know if you want to cancel.

Contact Utilities

You should contact utility companies for two reasons. One is to make sure that all utility assessments have been paid for any new project. For example, local governments may charge a *tie-in* fee for your development to connect to the storm sewer system. If the developer does not pay the fee, it becomes a lien against the property. Other utilities might have assessments for moving water lines to accommodate new roads, moving power poles because the contours of the property have changed, and other such matters.

The other reason you want to contact utilities is to make sure all the services you will need are available in the area, and to begin making arrangements to turn on the utilities in your name. Some utility companies will handle things over the phone for you, while others will require you to appear in person to sign forms. You do not want all of this to wait until the last minute. Additionally, some lenders require proof of adequate utility service, which means you will have more forms to deliver to the closing agent.

Chapter 17:
The Closing

You have your unit picked out, you have a contract, you have a loan commitment, the down payment is in the bank, the due diligence is finished, and all documents are where they are supposed to be. You are ready for the closing.

By federal law, you may require that an estimated settlement sheet, showing all costs and expenses, be provided to you by the day before closing, at the latest. The timely production of an estimated settlement sheet is not automatic, so you must be sure to request it. The afternoon of closing is no time to find out you will need to find another $1,200 to bring to the closing table.

When you go to the closing, you will probably see a conference table with many stacks of paper, all of which seem to require signatures and initials. It can be a little intimidating, but take your time and ask the right questions, and it will go smoothly. This chapter points out some of the things that may require additional questions on your part.

INSIDER TIP:

Even in a law firm, real estate closings are generally prepared by a team of secretaries, legal assistants, and paralegals. Almost every single scrap of paper is a form that comes off the computer. Do not be bashful about asking for copies of the forms ahead of time, with blank spaces instead of your particular information. That way you can read them and ask questions instead of feeling pressured to simply sign your name without reading.

Closing Procedures

Depending on the part of the country in which you live, closings are handled a couple of different ways. If you have an attorney, he or she will take care of these matters with the closing agents and explain the documents to you. If you are doing it on your own, this discussion gives a general outline of what to expect.

The closing agent will already have all the information and documents you previously supplied, including the sales contract. Your lender will send the closing agent a loan package with the amount borrowed, note terms, interest rate, and any fees or expenses charged by the lender. Depending on the market, the lender might prepare the promissory note and mortgage, deed of trust, or security agreement, or sometimes the closing agent does this from provided software. The note is your promise to repay the loan. For condos or townhomes, the lender will need a mortgage or a deed of trust (depending on what state you are in) to take a lien on the unit. Because you are buying shares of stock with a co-op purchase, rather than real estate, the lender will take a security interest in the stock and your proprietary lease.

The lender will also send a list of requirements to be met before closing can take place. Usually, these requirements consist of documents that need to be signed and various proofs—such as proof of insurance—that must be supplied by the buyer.

Shortly before closing, the closing agent will receive a certified check from the lender, in the full amount of your loan without any deductions for points, origination fees, and so on. There are usually many other lender-related forms having to do with disclosures required by federal law.

In his or her research regarding the title, the closing agent might discover judgments or liens against people with names similar to yours or the seller's. If that happens, the closing agent may require proof that you are not the person with the judgment. He or she will require *name affidavits*, in which you represent, under oath, that you are not that person.

Most states allow repair or construction people to file liens against property for unpaid services. As a result, the closing agent will ask the seller to sign forms saying there have not been any repairs within the last six months or so (depending on your state's time limits), or all repairs have been paid in full.

You, as the buyer, will have to sign a lot of forms agreeing that everything possible has been disclosed to you, you have read every single page of every single document, and you have no unanswered questions. While there are numerous forms being placed in front of you for a quick signature, remember that these forms do hold up in court. Any clause you are asked to initial is something that is especially important, because, sometime in the past, somebody got sued over that clause.

Do not let anybody rush you through a closing. If the closing agent wants your initials, ask him or her to explain what the clause means, plus an example of when it might become important. Make the person slow down and speak clearly. He or she may have done three thousand closings, but this could be your first. As a practical matter, any language you object to is probably nonnegotiable at that point. The most comprehensive paragraphs try to prevent you from suing the lender, the title company, or the real estate agent if anything goes wrong—even if it is really their fault. As always, decide how much risk you want to live with, enter the future forewarned about what sort of risks to avoid, and move on with the closing.

The Settlement Statement

If you borrow money to complete the closing, your lender is supposed to supply you with an estimated settlement statement within three days of your application. It is just a good faith estimate, and generally includes only loan-related expenses and costs. Federal law also requires lenders to give you something called the Special Information Booklet, which explains your rights under the *Real Estate Settlement and Procedures Act* (RESPA, pronounced "ress-puh").

The settlement statement is usually prepared on a form prepared by the Department of Housing and Urban Development (HUD). This form is called a HUD-1. It must account for all money changing hands at closing, all credits, fees, and expenses of the closing, any loans, and the distribution of all loan money. Some expenses might be noted on the HUD-1 with an amount in parentheses, and the notation *POC*. That means "paid outside closing," and represents additional bills that have already been paid or that will have to be paid after closing. Sometimes a home inspection or other such minor items will be POC. As a practical

INSIDER TIP:

A little gentle pressure can help get things done on time. Four days before the scheduled closing, call the closing agent and ask what date and time you can expect to receive your settlement statement, which will be on the form entitled "HUD-1." Call again two days before closing. Insist that you will pick up the HUD-1 at his or her office, if at all possible. Faxed copies of these legal-sized documents, reduced to letter-sized paper, are usually unreadable, as are PDF scans.

matter, most professionals performing services in connection with a home loan prefer to give their bills to the closing agent so they are assured of being paid in a timely manner.

Remember, everybody makes mistakes now and then. Review the settlement statement carefully to make sure expenses are allocated properly between buyer and seller according to your contract terms. In addition, keep a sharp eye for missing items, such as real estate tax prorations or dues prorations.

A *proration* is something that is split proportionately. If association dues are paid on the first of each month, but you close on the 15th, then you will owe the seller a refund for half of that month's dues—if you agreed to do so in the contract and if the dues have in fact been paid. Real estate taxes are generally paid in arrears. An owner who sells on June 30th, in a jurisdiction that assesses real estate taxes on December 31st, will owe half a year of taxes—but you will have to write a check for the whole amount in December. You should receive a credit on the settlement statement for six months of accrued taxes, if your contract provides for that. If the contract is silent, you will just have to pay for the whole year when December rolls around.

Other Closing Documents and Procedures

You will be asked to sign a *Foreign Investment in Real Property Tax Act (FIRPTA) affidavit*. Congress was concerned that foreign sellers would sell their property and not pay any income taxes on the sale proceeds. As a result, the Act required that buyers withhold 10% of the purchase price and pay it over to the IRS. The seller could then apply to the IRS for a refund, if one was due. This caused an incredible number of headaches, though, so the IRS allows a huge loophole. If the buyer signs an affidavit saying the purchase price is less than $300,000, or the buyer has current good faith plans to live in the property at least 50% of the time, then no one has to work with the IRS withholding issues. Your plans can change the day after closing, and that is all right—as long as you are being truthful about your intentions the day you sign the affidavit.

Some condominium associations and co-op apartments require that they be given the first chance to buy units coming on the market. It is rare for them to exercise that right, but your closing company may require a *waiver of right of first refusal.* Although this does not technically require your signature, some companies will require your initials.

Almost always, the title company or closing agent will record your deed for you, because it is writing the title insurance, and it is in its best interest to make sure your deed gets recorded before any possible judgment or lien against the seller. In most states, if you close on Friday afternoon and the IRS records a lien against the seller on Monday afternoon, and then your deed is recorded on Tuesday morning, the IRS can seize your unit. Title insurance will have to pay off the IRS and then try to find your seller for reimbursement. This is why it is a good idea to record deeds right away. Be sure to ask who records the deed.

No matter who records your deed, you will have to change the property tax assessments into your own name. Take care of this right away. You might be entitled to valuable homestead, senior citizen, or other tax discounts that could be lost if you do not file for them immediately.

Deductible Closing Expenses

Make a copy of every single closing document. The originals should stay in a file you have prepared for that particular property. A copy will go in a file for preparation of your current year's tax returns. Some expenses can be deducted in your current year's income, and others can be deducted proportionately over several years. State laws may vary, but a breakdown of common items and their tax treatment under IRS regulations is included on page 200.

Column A is for items that can be deducted in the same year as your purchase. Column B items must be divided by the number of years in your loan, and only that amount may be deducted each year. Column C items can be added to your basis—the amount you paid for your unit— and have the effect of increasing your purchase price when you need to calculate profit on a sale.

Tax Deductions for Home Purchase Expenses

	A	B	C
Loan origination fee for primary home purchase	✔		
Buyer-paid loan discount points for primary home purchase	✔		
Seller-paid loan discount points for primary home (but only if the seller does not deduct them also)	✔		
Any of the above three, but for a secondary home		✔	
Prepaid interest	✔		
Property tax prorates	✔		
Title insurance for owner			✔
Survey			✔
Legal fees for closing			✔
Recordation fees and transfer taxes			✔
Normal seller expenses you agree to pay, like real estate commission, back taxes, etc.			✔

Consult IRS Publications 530, "Tax Information for First Time Homeowners"; 523, "Selling Your Home"; 587, "Business Use of Your Home"; and, 936, "Home Mortgage Interest Deduction." They are all available at **www.irs.gov** or by calling 800-829-3676.

Chapter 18:
Ownership Responsibilities

Congratulations! You are a new homeowner and a new member of a community. The community will benefit you socially and economically, but will also require some responsibilities from you. If you are knowledgeable about the things expected from you, and you perform them conscientiously, you should have a long and pleasant experience with your choice of housing.

Participate in Governance

Your building or development is a mini-country with its own rules, regulations, and ways of doing things. The governing body is the homeowners or condo association, or the co-op board. This body can do pretty much whatever it wants as long as it has the votes and as long as no one's civil rights are being violated. Do not think of it as some sort of benevolent group handling all the grunt work no one else wants. Unless you are fond of unpleasant surprises, you must

INSIDER TIP:

In one college town, the owners of condos near a football stadium voted to exclude students. It turned out that only the wealthiest people, who simply wanted a place during football season, could use the units. Many parents had to sell their units, because they could no longer justify the expense through decreased housing costs for their college-age children.

attend meetings, vote, and keep yourself informed in the between-times. Remember, too, that you have talents and insights that can benefit everyone else, if you are willing to share your thoughts.

There are some basic rules for how any meeting should be run. Usually, the larger the group, the more formal the rules. In a large enough group, the meetings may need to follow guidelines established in the Bylaws or use the *Robert's Rules of Order*. These rules can be rather complex and technical, but they exist to make sure there is order during meetings, and that everyone has the opportunity to be heard. You can consult **www.robertsrules.com** for more information. Some general rules you should know and follow include the following.

- ◆ Know how many votes it takes to do certain things. Some votes require a simple majority, while others require two-thirds acceptance. You can find this in the Bylaws.

- ◆ Ask that agenda items have scheduled start times. Taking too long on routine things so that you never have time for the problems is not good practice.

- ◆ Use a *point of order* objection when speakers are heard in the wrong order. The chair must recognize speakers in alternating order—for and against the motion.

- ◆ A *call for the question* does not mean all discussion must stop immediately. It is merely a strong recommendation by someone that discussion be reined in after a few more speakers, because the movant feels the arguments are becoming repetitive and wasting time. No one is obligated to stop talking, though, simply because someone has called for the question.

- ◆ After a motion has been made, restated by the chair, and seconded by someone else, you can move to amend the motion. You do this by suggesting words to be added or deleted. There is then discussion and a vote on your amendment before returning to the main issue, when another motion to amend can be made. This is a good way to narrow down a dangerous motion until it is relatively harmless.

Manage the Management Company

A great number of condos, townhome projects, and co-op apartments hire third-party management companies to handle the routine work. This routine work would be things like collecting dues, arranging for various goods and services, maintaining quality control, paying bills, and performing certain accounting functions. Just because someone else is doing all these things does not mean you do not have to think about them, or about the management company that is doing them. Third-party management companies are the hired help, and must be managed just like any other employees. Make sure they do their job properly. Depending on the particulars of the management contract, they should:

  ◆ collect and account for all association dues and assessments;

  ◆ report any dues or assessments more than thirty days past due to the association governing body, and to the membership as a whole, with a recommendation for enforcement action;

  ◆ audit all bills and affirm that they are accurate, the work was performed properly, and there are no offsets;

  ◆ identify all vendors who offer a discount for early payment, and pay bills in time to take advantage of the discounts;

  ◆ pay all other bills within twenty days of receipt;

  ◆ generate a letter to the vendor, with copies to the members, explaining why any bills not paid within twenty days of receipt bill are not being paid in a timely manner;

  ◆ put all service and maintenance contracts out for bids to at least three comparable companies, and report the results to the board for decision annually;

  ◆ annually prepare a budget for the coming year, as well as a report concerning capital expenditures expected within the next five years, so the membership can take appropriate action;

  ◆ keep a log of nonconforming uses, complaints, and requests for repairs, which will be available for inspection by any member of the association; and,

  ◆ report quarterly to the homeowners, via a newsletter, regarding anticipated changes in the area that might affect property values in the condominium project.

You might have other ideas for managing the managers. Whatever you require, it is essential to be diligent in making sure the responsibilities are being handled properly. As the old saying goes, "Inspect what you expect" and life will be much easier.

Understand Your Community Personality

Your considerations when voting on dues, assessments, and improvements depend on whether your condominium development is primarily vacation, full-time residential, investment for resale, or investment for rental property. If you can evaluate the personality of the group, you can understand its hot buttons and perhaps create alliances or compromises to get things accomplished. Every circumstance is different, but general rules are as follows.

- ◆ Vacation condo owners prefer lower dues with future repairs to be met by assessment, because most vacation condo owners know they will not own their unit when the roof needs to be repaired—they will own something else. It will not be their problem, so they do not want to have to pay for it. If that is the primary market to buy your unit, keep the dues low. Sadly, for beachfront property in hurricane-prone areas, most people count on their insurance company to eventually be responsible for a new roof, landscaping, and so on.

- ◆ Vacation condo owners favor recreational improvements, but not overall quality of life improvements. If your facility appeals primarily to such owners, vote to spend money on tennis courts, pools, stables, or golf facilities. Avoid spending money on the latest telecommunications craze, faster elevators, or a doorman.

- ◆ Full-time residential owners generally take the long view and prefer higher dues over future large assessments, so vote accordingly. They also seek out quality of life amenities, such as security, child-friendly play areas, socializing opportunities, and convenience. Even if you, personally, are not a full-time residential owner, you have to think about resale value when voting on issues. Vote for things that will improve your ability to sell your unit in the future.

- Landlords prefer higher dues and decreased possibility of future assessments. In other words, landlords would prefer to build up reserves for future expenses like a new roof, rather than simply have an assessment when it is time for a new roof, because they can adjust their rental charges to cover dues, but it is hard to recoup the expense of an assessment.
- Landlords want any improvements to justify higher rents. If they cannot charge a higher rent because of a particular improvement (pool, exercise room, and so on), then they will not vote for it.
- Investment-for-resale owners usually plan to flip their properties as soon as the capital gains period is reached. They usually do not want to spend any money on anything, unless it is an emergency, or unless it will dramatically increase unit values in a short period of time. If you are a full-time, long-term resident in a project dominated by investors, be prepared for a tough sales job to obtain approval for any improvements.

Vote Intelligently on Dues and Assessments

As a member of the association, or as a shareholder of the co-op, you have responsibilities to the group at large, including the responsibility to make wise decisions for the entire community—even if it might increase your expenses somewhat. Your number one responsibility is to preserve and improve property values. If you own a detached home in the country, you can neglect that responsibility because you will be the only one harmed. In a condo or townhome project, or in a cooperative apartment, you do not have the same freedom.

Over the course of your ownership, you will probably have opportunities to vote on dues increases, assessments, or other financial changes, such as the imposition of a transfer fee when a unit is sold. Each time the subject comes up, you should ask yourself the following questions. (Not all will be relevant to every situation.)

- *Will this decision save the group money or cost more money in the long run?* Do you fix the roof one more time, or is it finally time to replace it? Will new landscaping plants be more maintenance-free and more drought-tolerant, reducing water and lawn care expenses? Do you increase dues slightly in order to build up reserves, or do you wait and impose assessments later?

◆ *Do we sacrifice anything by making this decision?* This usually arises in the context of failing to increase dues every year. However, all your expenses increase every year. You either need to keep pace or you need to cut services—which will it be?

◆ *Will this expenditure pay for itself by increasing property values?* If a new roof and new landscaping cause an assessment of $3,000 per unit, will the enhanced curb appeal increase the value of each unit by more than $3,000?

◆ *If support for this new amenity is not 100%, is there another way to pay for it?* About 60% of the owners would like a fitness center, but all of them agree it will not increase property values. Is it possible to pay for it through a specialized membership and monthly dues program?

◆ *Does this place an unreasonable burden on some members?* Can absolutely necessary assessments be spread out on a payment plan? Should there be a grace period of a year or so before transfer fees go into effect, so no one has any surprises?

Each situation will raise its own questions. As a general rule, you should ask yourself if the issue under consideration is fair and financially prudent. When there seems to be a conflict between fairness and prudence, you must come down on the side of fiscal responsibility, and then figure out some way to lessen the effects of any potential unfairness.

Avoiding Problems

Buying a condo, townhome, or co-op apartment is like getting married—you should not plan on making any dramatic changes to the other party in order to make your life better or easier. The rules are in place, the monthly fees cannot be modified very much, and sometimes the neighbors are going to be a little bit noisy—that is just life in a community. Remember your grammar school report card scores for "works and plays well with others." If you remember this important skill, you will do fine in most situations.

The other important thing to remember is that if you are going to be a troublemaker and complain about every tiny rules infraction by your neighbors, someone is going to start aiming for you. Practice some common sense, and try to resolve differences with your neighbors directly before reporting them to the association or the board.

Proper Management of Rental Units

While many people buy condos with the intent to rent them out for all or part of the year, sometimes owners unexpectedly find themselves renting as a result of changes in personal circumstances or market conditions. If you are away for an extended period of time traveling or working, you may have to rent out your unit to help cover costs. In some cases, condo owners must rent out their units rather than sell, because the market has declined and the market value is now less than the mortgage. Whether you are an intentional or an accidental landlord, you still need to exercise the same care when renting out your unit.

Before considering renting your unit, make sure you are allowed to rent it. Many condominium Bylaws forbid rentals. Others charge a large *impact fee* that could change the economics of the situation for you, so rentals no longer make sense. Some local governments also charge a residential rental tax.

If you own a unit in a vacation condominium development and want to enjoy short-term rentals, the owners' association or the management company will probably be able to help you. They can handle advertising, showings, rentals, and payments, and they can provide general property management services. At a minimum, all vacation-rental management contracts should contain the following provisions.

- ◆ The management company is responsible for screening all tenant applicants as to creditworthiness, criminal history, and references from prior landlords.
- ◆ The management company must adhere to a collections schedule agreed by you, and not allow tenants to be more than thirty days delinquent on their monthly rent. You might want to require that daily or weekly rentals be paid in advance, just like a hotel.

- The management company must perform a physical inspection of the property at least once a month (or more often, if you have daily or weekly rentals) and promptly report all damage.
- List and schedule the reports you will receive.
- List all services included in the regular fee, and list additional services available and at what cost.
- List emergency telephone numbers for management and maintenance personnel.
- Include any rental restrictions, such as prohibitions against pets, smokers, three or more unrelated people, and anything else allowed by law.

If you need to rent out your unit for a year or more, or you do not live in a vacation condo, you may be on your own and unable to find specialized condo management companies. As an alternative, you can contact some of the management companies that handle apartments and rental houses. Make sure you have the same provisions listed above, except you also want to specify the shortest term rental you will accept.

Otherwise, you will need to find and screen tenants, work out the terms of the lease, collect the rents, and make sure your tenant is maintaining the unit. There is nothing peculiar to condos in this situation, except the following—you remain responsible to the association for your tenant's actions. If the association forbids holiday decorations past January 1ˢᵗ, but your tenant leaves blinking lights in the window through March, you could be liable. You cannot blame it on the tenant. You have to control the tenant or suffer the consequences in fines, penalties, nasty letters, or any other pressure the association has at its disposal.

Buy a standard book about being a landlord and follow its advice. Under no circumstances should you rent your unit without a signed, written lease. Even if the lease is to your little sister for $1 per month, get it in writing. Many families have ended up in court over misunderstandings on handshake deals.

Make sure any lease has the following additional provision.

Tenant agrees to abide by all covenants, conditions, restrictions, rules, and any other requirements of the condominium association, as fully as if Tenant owned the unit himself or herself. If Tenant engages in any behavior or activities that expose Landlord to liability for fines, penalties, assessments, court action, attorney's fees, or anything else at all, then Tenant agrees to indemnify Landlord and hold Landlord harmless. Any such activities as described above will constitute a default if not cured within twenty-four hours of notice to Tenant, and may result in Landlord's exercise of all its remedies.

In addition, check with your neighbors periodically to see what they think about your tenants. This is a community, after all, and what your neighbors think can have major consequences to your bank account if they choose to fine you for your tenant's actions.

You will also need to purchase special absentee owner's insurance to cover liability and possible property damage. A security deposit will help reduce the likelihood of tenant damage, but you need to expect more wear and tear on the unit than might occur if you were occupying it yourself. A security deposit will help reduce the likelihood of tenant damage. Try to get two months' rent, but realize that some states prohibit deposits greater than one month's rent. Be aware that even the best tenant will not care for your property as well as you would, and price your rent accordingly.

Miscellaneous Considerations

Remember, you own a piece of the condo's common areas. That is *your* locker room with mold growing in the grout—would you tolerate that inside your bathroom? If you live in a co-op apartment, remember that you own stock in a corporation, just like IBM or Krispy Kreme. Anything you can do to make that corporation financially healthy and desirable to new stockholders is going to help you out as well. Townhome residents enjoy significant savings through the use of party walls, but must be good neighbors in order to attract good neighbors. All in all, if you remember that you are a member of a community, and you owe some amount of loyalty and responsibility to that community above yourself, then you will make the right decisions.

Chapter 19:
Thinking Ahead to a Sale of Your Condo

No matter what long-term plans you have today, eventually you are going to sell your home, or your heirs will do it for you. On average, homeowners today turn over once every seven to ten years, according to the most recent statistics from the National Association of Realtors. Whether you are purchasing your dream home or merely a stepping stone to something else, the odds are that you will sell or otherwise dispose of it sometime in the relatively near future. If you make the right decisions early, you improve the odds of maximizing financial success later.

Buy What You Can Afford

One school of thought says you should buy your second home first. In other words, buy more home than you can comfortably afford, and grow into it. This is not recommended, however. Instead, choose a price range in which you can place a reasonable down payment, and a mortgage for which you can make monthly payments that will pay off your loan in fifteen to twenty years. There are several reasons for this.

If the economy turns down temporarily, your equity gives you a cushion—you might lose some of it, but at least you will be able to sell and keep some of the money afterwards. People mortgaged to the hilt will probably end in foreclosure or bankruptcy. Next, if you need every penny every month for living expenses and loan payments, you simply will not be able to afford periodic repairs or upgrades. Your property will suffer *deferred maintenance* and will decline in value or at least not keep up with growth generally. As another consideration, some 100% financing, interest-only loans have clauses requiring large principal reductions if the property value declines below the loan balance. A temporary recession could have economically fatal consequences if you do not have the money demanded by the lender. You might have to place your home on the market for a quick sale, which will further depress the value.

Buy Smart to Sell Smart

An old saying in real estate is, "You make your profit when you buy, not when you sell." In other words, the most important factor is making a wise purchase decision, not having an aggressive and imaginative sales campaign. Even if they make no difference to you, personally, you must evaluate school districts, the proximity of retail and dining opportunities, distances from major employers, ease of access onto major traffic arteries, local government services and crime control, and the impact of environmental concerns such as pollution and scenery. The vast majority of future buyers will care about these things.

You should not disregard opportunities that might be a little substandard in some or all of the above categories, but go into the purchase with your eyes open and a realization that you will need to overcome those deficiencies in some other way when it comes time for resale. Perhaps you buy at a bargain price and then sell at a bargain price, but still make an acceptable profit. Maybe your unit has other selling features and an imaginative sales campaign would work.

For the most part, though, stick with safer choices if you plan to resell within the next five years or so. If you are worried about the impact of competition on your resale opportunities, then do what you can to limit that. Suppose there are twelve condo projects within one square mile, all with the same size units and the same recreational facilities. Obviously, all of them enjoy the same area amenities such as schools and retail opportunities. They all have pretty much the same décor. Does it matter which one you choose?

Yes, it does. Say one development has a small convenience store as a tenant on the ground floor. This adds nothing to the monthly expenses, but it is a valuable feature that makes this project stand out from the others. *Product differentiation* is a time-tested and well-respected marketing tool. For future buyers who care about such an amenity, you will have no competition. Absent that feature, you are competing with everyone in the other eleven developments at the same level, trying to capture buyers. When products have nothing to distinguish themselves from each other (real or imagined), they have to compete on price alone.

Remember, however, that most amenities add to the monthly maintenance fees. Just as when you are voting on dues and assessments, you must evaluate the cost of a feature versus how much it will add to resale value. Future buyers may also be sensitive to recurring expenses, so you must strike a balance here.

Most advisors recommend you buy at the low end of a market rather than the high end. In other words, a somewhat modest development in an area of luxury homes will see its value pulled upwards by its neighbors. A unit with hardwood floors, granite counters, gourmet appliances, and designer plumbing fixtures will never retain its value in a building of homes with economy carpeting, laminate counters, kitchenettes, and utilitarian bathrooms. This is the wrong kind of product differentiation.

Know the Neighbors

Try to buy in a development of people with similar goals. If you plan to live in your unit, then you want a large number of owner-occupants rather than landlords renting to tenants. You will have similar concerns when voting on issues. As one example, upwardly mobile high turnover owner-occupants will favor low monthly fees with the possibility of large future assessments (hopefully after they have sold), while retirees and landlords prefer predictable monthly dues and no surprises in the future. Consider that vacationers are not interested in installing exercise facilities, updating the landscaping, or banding together to lobby against zoning changes next door.

All successful real estate agents approach the neighbors first for leads on potential buyers. For investment properties, the people who own neighboring properties might want to add your own to their portfolio. Residents know people of similar interests and financial ability. The easiest sales always start with the neighbors.

MYTHBUSTER

A real estate broker can value your home

Real estate brokers are not licensed appraisers and are not allowed to tell you the value of your home. They can recommend an asking price, but most lack the experience or sophistication to evaluate that properly. Unfortunately, it is a common practice for real estate agents to tell you a very high price so they can get the listing, or a very low price so they can sell quickly and look like a hero. Your best protection is to have a good idea of your own regarding the market value of similar units.

Stay Informed about Your Market

Once you buy, you cannot stop shopping. Throughout your ownership, you will need to stay informed about other condos, townhomes, or co-ops in your general part of town, and about sale prices for detached housing. All of these other properties are the competition when it comes time for you to sell. If you have a good feeling for price and market trends, you can make informed decisions about when to sell and how much to ask.

The other reason you need to keep track of nearby communities and what they are doing is because you want to vote intelligently at your meetings. If every other co-op within ten blocks is getting a password-protected Web page for its tenants so they can log in for news, updates, financial info, and reporting of maintenance problems, consider doing the same thing in your co-op. If you do not take reasonable steps to keep up with your competition, then you will be at a resale disadvantage down the road. You might form a *competition committee* to be in charge of this market research. You can suggest it at the next meeting and volunteer to be the chairman. This is a great way to get into the heart of community governance and bypass all the existing cliques.

Deciding Whether to Remodel

You may decide to buy a bargain property and then remodel it upwards to fit the market and become more valuable. Generally speaking, painting and fixing up is the cheapest remodel and returns the highest profit.

Most buyers are simply unable to look past orange walls, badly soiled carpeting, and dingy cabinets to see a diamond in the rough.

If you plan to do more aggressive remodeling, there is some help for you regarding improved resale values. Not surprisingly, how much your resale value improves depends on your part of the country and your particular neighborhood. For example, according to the National Association of Realtors' "2005 Cost vs. Value Report," upgrading windows will increase value by 103% of their cost in the West, but only 83.7% of their cost in the South. You might want to check out the entire report by ordering it online at **www.realtorreprints.com** at a cost of $6.50, or by calling 717-399-1900 extension 166. Your particular neighborhood or development might have its own general rules. Before thinking about spending tens of thousands of dollars improving a property, be sure to prepare an estimated remodeling budget and compare it to the increased value you think you will realize.

Recouping Your Investment and Closing Costs

As a general rule, any property must increase in value by about 10% in order to recoup the expenses of buying and selling. This can vary, depending on the percentage commission charged by a listing real estate agent. In addition, most co-ops and some condos charge a flip tax or transfer fee, which could be a flat fee, a percentage of the sale price, a percentage of the profit, or some combination of those.

When buying a condo, you will also have to pay escrows for taxes and insurance. These are considered normal costs of home ownership and so are not included in the calculations, any more than you would include the power and water bills.

Use the worksheet on page 217 to calculate your profit on a potential sale. For purposes of this worksheet, the assumption is that you will not have any remodeling expenses. If you anticipate remodeling expenses, you will need to add those dollars to the chart. Closing costs vary widely in different parts of the country. Ask a real estate agent or your mortgage company to help you fill in some of these blanks for a typical unit in your price range. Also, find out how the closing expenses are typically shared. It is always a matter of individual negotiation, but usually the buyer and seller split the cost of title insurance and closing expenses, for example, but not expenses related to obtaining a loan. (For more information on closing costs, see Chapter 17.)

In addition, you might want to find out about transfer taxes. These can range up to 5% of the sale price, and are usually the seller's legal responsibility, although you can negotiate for reimbursement by the buyer. The "Other" item could include things not directly related to a sale or purchase, but related to moving. You have to factor in those expenses if you do not have to sell but are trying to decide if the time is right for a sale.

Add together all the numbers on the "Purchase" side. That is your gross purchase expense. Next, start with the "Sale Price" on the "Sale" side, and then subtract all the numbers that come afterwards. That is your net sales proceeds. Subtract the gross purchase expense from the net sale proceeds.

Will you make a profit? If not, how long do you have to hold your unit before you can break even? Use the worksheet on page 218 to calculate that.

Calculating Profit on the Sale of a Condo, Townhome, or Co-op

PURCHASE		SALE	
Purchase price		Sale price	
Loan origination fees		Title	
Survey		Document preparation	
Environmental inspection		Closing fees and expenses	
Home inspection		Transfer taxes	
Appraisal		Condo association transfer fees	
Credit check		Real estate commission	
Termite and moisture bonds		Other:	
Title insurance			
Document preparation			
Closing fees and expenses			
Document recording fees			
Condo association transfer fees			
Other:			
Gross Purchase Expense		Net Sale Proceeds	

How Long Must You Own Your Condo
Before You Can Make a Profit on Sale?

YOUR WORKSHEET		EXAMPLE
Purchase price		$100,000
Total purchase expenses		$4,000
Total sale expenses		$8,000
Total purchase and sale expense		$12,000
Estimated annual market appreciation		6% per year
Percentage appreciation needed to break even*		12%
Years needed before you will break even**		2 years

*** Percentage Appreciation Needed to Break Even =
Total Purchase and Sales Expense ÷ Purchase Price**
(Example: $12,000/$100,000 = 0.12 or 12%)

**** Years Needed Before You Will Break Even =
Percentage Appreciation Needed to Break Even ÷
Estimated Annual Market Appreciation**
(Example: 12%/6% = 2 years)

All this is important now because if you are trying to decide between two different properties, and you know your job will probably transfer you in two years, you might want to evaluate which one has the best likelihood of rapid price escalation in order to recover all your expenses and either break even or make a profit in two years.

Investing in Rental Properties

There is simply not enough room here to cover all the basic investing tools you need to use and the advice you should follow in investing in rental property. Buy a good book that seems to reflect your personal philosophy. You might be a conservative investor, buying for the long-term, or you might want to buy and sell properties every few years. Low-income housing, luxury properties, student housing, and corporate housing for high-level transients all have different strategies, drawbacks, and opportunities. There is not one book that will cover everything for all investors. Think about your goals and your own strengths and weaknesses, read the reviews, and spend some time online or in a bookstore flipping through different books. Buy one that matches you, and read it cover to cover. You will be happy with the investment in time and money.

Depending on your city, be sure to investigate any rent control or rent stabilization laws in effect or planned for the near future. While may people think of New York City in that regard, many other cities have similar laws. This can have serious consequences for any investing decisions.

Estate Planning Issues

Those of you who plan to buy your dream home and live in it forever still need to think about a few transfer issues. General estate planning is far outside the scope of this book, but you do have to consider association Bylaws, restrictions, and expenses when making gifts in your will. If your complex restricts residency to people over the age of 55, for example, your 48-year-old daughter may be saddled with the economic burdens of ownership but none of the benefits. In that circumstance, you might not want to have her on your title as a co-owner for a probate avoidance tool, because it could cause other problems worse than probate. You may need to talk to a lawyer about other avenues of estate planning.

Many people purchase estate planning kits that tell them how to set up specialized trusts in order to avoid estate taxes. Be aware that vacation condos rented out to others during part of the year might not qualify for such favorable tax treatment. Currently, the owner must actually occupy his or her condo for fourteen days per year, or a time equivalent to 10% of the days it is rented to someone else, whichever is greater. The rent must be at fair market value—you cannot rent it to the grandchildren for $1 a day. In addition, rental activities must be handled by someone else.

Contrary to popular belief, vacation condos do qualify for the estate planning tool called a *qualified personal residence trust*. Basically, you transfer your unit into a trust with your named heirs as beneficiaries. You retain the right to live in or otherwise use the unit during your lifetime. However, this is a tricky area of the law. Do not attempt to do it yourself—seek professional advice. Also, you must make sure that such transactions do not violate the Rules or Bylaws of the condominium association.

Flipping

It is not a recommended practice, but *condo flipping* is a way some people make money. In the typical situation, an investor will reserve as many units as he or she can afford before construction begins. The investor will pay a relatively small reservation fee or deposit for each one. In hot markets, with good properties, the price of each unit will usually increase several times before construction is even completed. The goal of the flipper is to sell the purchase contract at a tremendous profit before the project is finished. In other words, the investor never has to actually own the unit—just the right to buy the condo.

If the flipper signs a contract to buy ten units at $350,000 each, he or she might put down a 5% deposit, for a total of $175,000. According to the plan, it might take one year to complete construction. With any luck, in one year those same units will be worth $700,000 each. The flipper can sell his or her contracts for $317,500 each, which represents a $300,000 profit plus the initial $17,500 deposit per unit. Each new owner will be able to buy a unit for the original $350,000 contract price, making a total of $650,000 to buy something worth $700,000. The new owners are happy and the original flipper is happy—everyone is delighted as long as the boom continues.

That is the trick—will the boom continue, and will it continue at the same pace? If prices remain stable at $350,000 or even slightly more, the flipper has $3.5 million in enforceable real estate contracts with his or her signature. Those are not enforceable just against the developer—

they could well be enforceable against the flipper. At the least, the flipper will have to pay damages if he or she cannot come up with the money to complete closing.

The flipping craze is now so frenzied that investors can go to **www.condoflip.com** for a marketplace to buy, sell, and trade flip contracts for land they have never seen in states they have never visited. A lot of people are getting rich, but a lot of people are going broke, and a lot more will go broke in the future. Buy a home because it makes sense, pay a reasonable price under current market conditions, but do not get greedy and head out to the flipping market.

Overcoming Analysis Paralysis

Analysis paralysis is a common affliction; do not be embarrassed. The symptoms include the desire to obtain *just one more piece of information* before making a decision. Of course, once gained, that information raises additional questions. At the end, how can you be sure sure you are making the right decision?

You cannot. Surprises happen, things get overlooked, life gets in the way of doing everything perfectly. The analysis paralysis disease cannot be cured, but the condition can be managed, allowing you a long and happy life. You have started out right, buying and reading this book all the way to the end. Now, write down your goals. Make a list of additional educational tools you need, and select one book or one mentor for each subject. Give yourself a deadline. After that, you should have a handle on the whole field of buying condos, co-ops, or townhomes to meet your goals.

Along the way, continue shopping in order to refine your knowledge of your particular market. When you find something that is right, you will know it. Do not talk yourself into a purchase, because you should usually listen to your instincts. By the same token, do not talk yourself out of something, either. Because of your investment in things like this book, you are way ahead of most other home buyers. Usually, nothing bad happens to *them*, and you are better prepared. Like weddings, something almost certainly will go wrong, but it is rarely fatal, no matter how catastrophic it seems at the time. Learn from the experience, drop me a line at **condos@bellsouth.net**, and pass on some advice to people in your life. You will be just fine.

Glossary

A

adjustable-rate mortgages (ARMs). The interest rate on your loan will change from time to time, usually called the adjustment period, as the market changes. The market is defined in the loan documents as being determined by something called an index. In other words, the note might say that if ten-year Treasury bonds increase by ½ of 1%, your interest rate will also increase that amount. When a lender offers you a fixed-rate mortgage, it is taking a risk that interest rates will not increase dramatically by the time you sell your home and pay off the loan. To compensate for that risk, they charge a slightly higher interest rate than adjustable rate mortgages. That is why you can usually obtain a cheaper rate with an ARM. Beware of extremely low ARM rates, though, because they may have a very short adjustment period and then a much higher interest rate, which could be determined by some sort of artificial index.

adjustment period. In lending, it is the time period during which an adjustable rate mortgage cannot increase or decrease. The adjustment period might be three months, meaning it can change every three months but no more often. Some adjustable rate mortgages do not have adjustment periods, and can increase or decrease as often as the market changes.

agent. In real estate, an agent is authorized to act on behalf of another person, called the principal or client. Agents owe their clients a very high degree of loyalty and confidentiality, and are required to put their clients' economic interests ahead of their own. Most real estate agents work for sellers as *direct agents* (the person with the relationship with seller) or *subagents* (other agents who interact with the direct agent, but probably have never met with or spoken to the client.) If you ask a real estate agent to help you find a home, and you do not have a written buyers' agency contract with that person, then in all likelihood they will act as a subagent for the seller and will not attempt to protect *your* best interests.

amortizing loans. Loans on which you make regular payments that will pay the accrued interest and reduce the loan amount. At the end of the amortization period, you will have paid the loan in full and owe nothing. This is different from *interest-only* loans, on which you may make principal reductions regularly, but are not required to do so. Amortizing loans are safest for most consumers, but will cause your monthly payments to be somewhat higher.

appraisal. An opinion of the value of real estate, offered by a trained a licensed professional appraiser. By law, anyone else offering an opinion regarding real estate is not allowed to call it an appraisal and is not allowed to call their opinion a *value.* Real estate brokers and agents offer opinions on *market price* and make recommendations on a selling price, but never a value.

arbitration. A method of settling disputes outside the traditional court system. In order to force arbitration, rather than a trial, the parties must have a written contract agreeing to submit their disputes to arbitration. The process is usually quick, informal, and designed to level the playing field between well-funded parties traditionally able to afford the best legal assistance, and consumers with little sophistication or financial resources. In exchange, the parties give up significant rights to discovery—finding out what the other sides knows—and to appeal in the case of errors.

assessments. Special amounts of money billed to owners from time to time for unusual expenses. Some communities charge slightly higher dues each month than necessary to cover operating expenses. The excess is then put in a fund to cover emergencies, unexpected repairs, or perhaps long-term expenses such as new roofs, repaving the parking lot, and so on. Other communities prefer to keep their monthly dues low, and then charge large assessments when problems arise. If the assessments are not paid, they become a lien on the homeowner's property and could result in foreclosure.

assumable loans. Traditionally, assumable loans were mortgage loans that could be taken over by the new owner of a property, without any credit check, underwriting, or additional fees except perhaps a minimal assumption fee. Those days are long gone. Today, some loans can be assumed with a minimum of costs, but the buyer still has to meet credit and other underwriting requirements just as if it were a new loan.

B

balance sheet. The accounting document that lists all of an entity's assets (money in the bank, dues that are owing but still unpaid, perhaps securities or other investments) and liabilities (money owed to suppliers, property taxes that will be due in the future, perhaps mortgage balances at a co-op). When reviewing a balance sheet, you want to see if there are any footnotes for *contingent liabilities,* which are things that might not come to pass, such as lawsuits, but should still be considered when evaluating the economic health of an organization. The balance sheet will tell you if the organization is paying its bills on time, if its collecting its dues on time, and if there is enough extra money on hand to cover repairs.

board of directors. The governing group in a co-op apartment. Under the Bylaws, the board of directors will be entitled to make some decisions without input from the other shareholder/tenants. You should read the Bylaws to see what things may be left to their discretion.

broker. In real estate, the broker is the person legally allowed to enter into a contract with a client regarding the purchase, sale, or leasing of real estate. Salespersons work under the broker. Usually, a salesperson obtains the listing on a property, or a salesperson brings the buyer to the closing table, and the broker has usually met neither one of these people. The law imposes tremendous responsibilities on the broker to train and supervise salespersons properly.

broker price opinion. An informal and inexpensive method of gaining a rough idea of market prices for similar properties. This is not an appraisal and cannot be relied on by a lender, nor can it usually be legally relied on by you if it turns out to be inaccurate.

C

cash flow statement. A financial document that tells you where an organization's cash is going each month. If a condo association or co-op board spends more cash than it takes in, you have to ask where the extra money is coming from to pay the bills. If they take in significantly more cash than they spend, you have to ask if some bills are not being paid, if it is building up a cash surplus, or what is going on. A cash flow statement should never be read by itself as an indication of financial health— you should always review the balance sheet, to discover unpaid liabilities, uncollected dues and cash reserves. You should also review the profit and loss statement to see if income and expense are roughly in equilibrium, without reference to collections issues.

cash vs. accrual. Different ways of doing an organization's accounting. Cash basis accounting for a condo association or co-op board would almost never be appropriate. With this type of accounting, income is counted when you collect it, and expenses are counted when you pay them. If you don't pay several bills, they just do not show up as expenses, even though they are truly liabilities that must be paid. If an organization uses cash basis accounting, it usually has something it wants to hide. Accrual basis accounting counts income when it is earned, and expenses when they are incurred. The swimming pool expenses will be summer-month expenses, even if the pool company does not get paid until December. With both types of accounting, you must also review the balance sheet to make sure there are not any outstanding bills as liabilities, and there are not any uncollected dues or assessments being counted as assets.

caveat emptor. Buyer beware! In some states, builders of new homes owe certain warranties to buyers, but sellers of used homes do not have to make any disclosures regarding defects and do not owe any warranties that things are in working order. In those states, the rule is caveat emptor—the buyer buys at his own risk.

common element. In a condominium project, anything not owned individually by individual unit owners. Common elements are owned by all owners, in common with each other. This would include lobbies, elevators, hallways, exterior walls, driveways and recreational or safety amenities. It would also include "your" front door, windows, balcony, exterior walls and possibly even "your" plumbing and wiring. Usually, the condominium documents will designate some common areas—such as a patio—as limited in usage to only one unit.

common interest development. A generic term for condominiums, cooperative apartments, and townhomes.

conditions, covenants, and restrictions. The condominium rules that spell out what is and is not allowed. Called CC&Rs for short. Sometimes townhome homeowners associations will also have Conditions, Covenants, and Restrictions.

condominium. A method of owning real estate so that some portion is owned individually, and everything else is owned in common with other people. In a small condominium project with one building and twenty units, each unit owner will own one-twentieth of the common elements such as hallways, building exterior, roof, etc. Many people think that the condominium association owns the common elements, but that is not true.

condominium association. The governing and enforcement mechanism in a condominium project. It does not own any of the real estate. This is different from a town home, in which the homeowners association is a separate legal organization that usually owns any common elements such as entrance signs and perhaps recreational amenities.

condotel. Usually a resort hotel in which individual rooms or suites are sold as condominium properties. A management company then rents the units out, much like a typical hotel property, but profits go to the unit owner.

conforming loans. Loans that conform to Fannie Mae and Freddie Mac underwriting guidelines. If a loan meets the guidelines, then Fannie Mae or Freddie Mac will buy the loan from your lender, package it with other loans, and sell the package to large investors.

contingencies. In contracts, things that must be satisfied before you will be obligated to purchase a property. A typical contingency would be financing contingency—if you cannot obtain acceptable financing, you are not obligated to go through with the purchase and may obtain a refund of your earnest money. Contingency are entirely a matter of negotiation, and can be anything the parties agree to.

conventional loans. Loans made by traditional lenders, as opposed to loans made by the government.

cooperative apartment. An apartment that can be rented only if you purchase stock in the company that owns the building. You still pay rent, but the amount is usually much less than rents for similar units in typical apartment buildings.

D

deed of trust. In some states, the method of holding real estate as collateral for a loan. In other states, an instrument called a mortgage is used. The differences between the two are largely a matter of historical accident and make no practical difference to the lender's rights or your responsibilities.

deferred maintenance. A term used to mean repairs have not been made in a timely manner, as needed. We might refer to a property as shabby, run-down, or needing some repairs to bring it up to expectations. Real estate professionals would say the property "has some deferred maintenance issues," because that is less emotional charged and accusatory than other expressions. It still means someone will want a discount off the asking price, but it is a more polite way of putting it.

discount brokers. Real estate brokers who do not offer the full range of traditional services such as advice, negotiations, screening prospects, and showing properties. Typically, discount brokers will give you placement in some sort of medium such as the Internet or the local multiple listing service. In return for the reduced services, they charge a discounted fee.

due diligence. The process of investigating a property to make sure it meets your needs, and has no hidden defects or drawbacks. The most common due diligence item is hiring a home inspector.

F

Fair Credit Reporting Act. Federal law that places restrictions on what information can be reported to other people about you, and what rights you have to correct erroneous information.

fiduciary duties. Special duties imposed by law on people because they are in a particular position or relationship that puts you at a disadvantage. The special duties generally involve a responsibility of absolutely loyalty, confidentiality and trust, and the necessity for the fiduciary to put his or her economic interests below that of the other party. Real estate brokers have fiduciary duties to their clients.

flip tax. Not a tax, but a fee imposed by some cooperative boards and condominium associations when a unit is sold. It can be a flat fee, a percentage of the sale price, a percentage of the profit, or some combination.

flipping. Buying with the intent to sell fairly quickly. In condominiums, flipping has come to mean the practice of making down payments on units under construction or even still in the early pre-construction phase, and then selling that contract to someone else. The flipper never takes title to the unit, and usually completes the transaction well before construction is even completed.

FSBO. For sale by owner. Pronounced fizz-boe.

H

HUD-1. Shorthand term for a real estate closing settlement statement, showing the amounts and sources of all money for the closing, allocation of fees, and expenses between buyer and seller, and the amount and payee of all funds disbursed.

J

joint tenants with right of survivorship. A way of holding title to real estate among two or more people. All owners have equal rights to the use of the property during their lifetimes, and the right to all of the property *if* they are the last survivor. As each joint tenant dies, his or her rights also die until the last one owns everything. Because of this technicality in how the survivor comes to own everything, no property changes hands at death and probate can be avoided.

L

land sale contract. Also called a bond for title or a deed for title. Does not have to be limited to land. A method of buying and financing real estate in which the buyer agrees to make payments to the seller, and the seller agrees to give the buyer a deed only at the end, when all the payments have been made. This is different from seller financing with a mortgage, in which the buyer receives a deed immediately but could lose the property through foreclosure if payments are not made on time. The laws gives fewer protections to buyers in a land sale contract, making it a very risky method of buying property.

leasehold condos and coops. Most of the time, a developer buys land, builds a condominium project, and then sells units to individual owners. Sometimes, a developer is not able to buy land (or perhaps a building scheduled for conversion), but can obtain it under a long term lease, usually for 99 years. Condominiums or co-op apartments on that property have rights only until the master lease expires. These are called leasehold condos or co-ops.

limited equity condos and coops. Subsidized housing that allows consumers with limited income to buy condos or co-ops. They obtain the property with little or no down payments and so have limited equity in them. When they sell, the sales prices is determined by a formula, not by market rates. As a result, the owners continue to have limited equity, because they are not able to build up equity through typical market appreciation, only through debt reduction as they make their monthly payments.

M

mansion tax. A tax imposed by New York City, and by the State of New Jersey, on sales of properties over a certain price. Currently, that number is $1,000,000, although there is tremendous pressure to increase this figure because one million dollars does not buy you much of a mansion any more. By law, the buyer pays the tax, but may negotiate in the sales contract for reimbursement by the seller.

mediation. A method of dispute resolution in which a knowledgeable and disinterested third party, usually a lawyer or retired judge, will assist parties in coming to a mutually agreeable solution to their problems. This is not binding, and an agreement to mediate does not impose any requirement to actually reach a compromise.

mortgage. A written instrument that gives a lender rights in real estate as collateral for a loan. Some states use a mortgage, some states use a deed of trust. There is little practical difference in the two.

mortgage banker. Someone who obtains pools of money from investors, and then loans that money out on mortgages. This is different from a mortgage broker, who acts as an intermediary between lenders and borrowers, but does not actually raise any money for loans.

mortgage broker. Someone who acts as in intermediary between lenders and borrowers, and assists the borrower in making choices among a variety of loan options.

N

negative amortization. The process of a loan's principal balance becoming higher over time rather than lower. This does not refer to accumulation of late charges and other such fees, but the actual principal balance, on which interest is calculated, becoming higher. Typically, this happens when someone obtains a loan which has an adjustable interest rate, but which guarantees that the monthly payments will not increase for some period of time. If the interest rate increases to the extent that the fixed monthly payments will not pay all of the interest, then the lender will pay itself the difference by "loaning" you more money and increasing the principal balance of your loan.

no-doc mortgage. Commonly used to refer to a loan that has no underwriting requirements. In reality, it means a mortgage loan that can be obtained even though the borrower cannot or will not provide any of the customary proofs of assets or income, such as tax returns, W-2s, or financial statements.

non-conforming loans. A loan that does not meet the underwriting requirements of Fannie Mae or Freddie Mac, either because of income levels, credit scores, or size of the loan.

P

party wall. A wall shared by two homeowners, such as in a town home development. Each owns the half of the all located on their land, but owes responsibilities to the other owner to keep the wall maintained sufficiently so each side is adequately supported.

payment caps. Some adjustable rate mortgages guarantee that monthly payments will not increase, or will not exceed a stated amount, even if interest rates climb dramatically. This can result in a situation called *negative amortization*, in which the principal balance of a loan increases over time instead of decreasing.

performance and completion bond. An insurance policy that typically protects a lender in the event a developer is unable to complete a project. If the developer defaults, the bond will pay enough money, up to policy limits, to hire someone else to complete the project.

periodic caps. In an adjustable rate mortgage, the maximum amount the interest rate can increase during any given period of time. For example, the note might provide that interest will not increase more than ½ of 1% per three-month period.

PITI. Shorthand for "principal, interest, taxes and insurance." Most people make monthly mortgage payments which include one month's interest, some amount of principal reduction, one-twelfth of the annual property insurance, and one-twelfth of the annual property taxes.

POC. Shorthand for "paid outside closing." A notation of POC on a settlement statement means that the particular expense is noted for informational purposes, but either has already been paid, or will need to be paid after closing. You should always ask about POC items to determine who is supposed to pay them—you might be surprised to learn it is you!

points—discount. A method of buying down your loan interest rate. One point is equal to 1% of the loan. Depending on interest rates, size of the loan, and general market competition, one point can reduce your interest rate by one-eighth of a percent to three-eighths of a percent.

points—origination. Fees charged in connection with a loan, but expressed in terms of a percentage of the loan rather than a flat fee. One point is equal to 1% of the loan. Typically there is a great deal of flexibility in negotiating origination points because they largely represent additional profit for the lender.

private mortgage insurance. A method of securing financing even if you do not have 20% of the purchase price to pay as a down payment. That equity supplies the safety net your lender needs in case it forecloses because it is extremely unlikely your unit will sell for less than 80% of your purchase price. If it does not have that protection, the lender will secure insurance to help protect it in case you default and the foreclosure sale of your unit is not enough to pay off the loan. The borrower pays the premiums for the insurance.

pro forma. A good faith estimate of financial conditions which will exist in the future. A developer will typically prepare a pro forma for a condominium project, showing anticipated expenses and monthly dues. If the pro forma is *revenue-neutral,* meaning expenses exactly match income, then you should wonder where the money will come from to pay unexpected repairs and infrequent but periodic items like roof replacement and landscape refurbishment.

profit and loss statement. An accounting document showing income and expenses over a period of time. Ideally, any profit and loss should show the current month, the year-to-date, and a comparison of these figures to the budget.

proprietary lease. The document that allows a co-op apartment owner to occupy a particular unit. Like ordinary leases, it spells out the rights and responsibilities of the parties, and the circumstances under which they can be deprived of their rights.

R

Real Estate Settlement and Procedures Act. Federal law that regulates how mortgage lenders interact with borrowers, and what information must be provided to borrowers so they can make informed decisions.

reserves. In accounting, funds built up in order to meet expenses that will come due in the future. A condominium association might charge slightly higher monthly dues than absolutely necessary in order to build up a reserve for roof replacement.

right of first refusal. Often confused with an *option* among consumers, but these are two separate things. A right of first refusal gives you the right to buy a property, but only if the owner offers it for sale to someone else. In that circumstance, it must be offered to you for the same price and terms, and you can elect to buy or to decline. An option is a right to buy property at some point in the future, even if the seller has no desire to sell at that time. Usually you pay a fee to purchase the option right; this is not earnest money, but a fee which is fully earned whether you buy or not.

S

security agreement. A document which gives lenders rights in non-real estate collateral. While a lender will have a *mortgage* or a *deed of trust* on real property, you will execute a security agreement to give it rights in the stock you purchase in a cooperative apartment building.

settlement statement. Document showing the amounts and sources of all money for the closing, allocation of fees and expenses between buyer and seller, and the amount and payee of all funds disbursed.

specific performance. A remedy for breach of contract, in which a court orders the defaulting party to perform its contract or risk going to jail for contempt of court. Typically, courts will grant specific performance to force defaulting sellers to go through with a sale. Traditionally, innocent sellers could obtain only monetary damages from defaulting buyers, but in rare circumstances courts will force purchasers to go through with their contract.

T

tenancy by the entireties. A method of holding title to real estate. It is available only in some states, and only for husbands and wives. They each own the property jointly for their lives, and then individually by the survivor. A divorce court cannot split the property between the spouses if they do not agree, and a creditor of one owner cannot force a sale of the property. Because of this, it is often used as an asset protection tool.

tenancy in common. A method of owning title to real estate, in which any number of owners share in the ownership. When one dies, his or her share passes to his or her heirs, not to the other owners. Commonly used by unrelated co-owners, or by spouses with children from prior marriages, who want their heirs to inherit the property rather than the other owners.

title insurance. Insurance policy that protects against defective ownership of real estate, such as claims of ownership by other parties, or claims of liens by creditors of the prior owners.

townhome. Sometimes refers to an architectural style of a two story home on a narrow lot, but more properly a legal concept of individual home ownership with a wall and perhaps a roof shared with the adjoining owner. Unlike a condo, the town home owner owns his or her own exterior walls, windows, doors, and yard.

transaction brokers. A type of real estate broker who assists in communications between buyers and sellers, and perhaps with facilitating a closing, but who does not represent any particular party.

Appendix:
Websites

The following websites are referenced in this book and may help you in various parts of your buying process.

www.caionline.org
    Community Associations Institute

www.communityassociations.net/state_laws.html
    State condo and coop laws

www.bankrate.com
    Many financial tools and advice for potential homebuyers

www.irs.gov/publications
    Publications explaining tax benefits of home ownership

www.ditech.com
    Many financial tools and advice for potential homebuyers

www.quickenloans.com
    Many financial tools and advice for potential homebuyers

www.annualcreditreport.com
    Order one free credit report, per agency, per year

www.gpoaccess.gov/uscode
  Obtain full text of any federal law

www.va.gov
  United States Veterans Administration

https://entp.hud.gov/idapp/html/hicostlook.cfm
  Current max on FHA insured loans

www.hud.gov
  U.S. Department of Housing and Urban Development:
  tools and advice

www.rurdev.usda.gov
  U.S. Department of Agriculture Rural Development loans

www.hud.gov/offices/pih/ih/homeownership/184
  Loan programs for Native Americans

www.realtor.org
  National Association of Realtors®

www.forsalebyowner.com
  Properties for sale by owners

www.homesbyowner.com
  Properties for sale by owners

www.homesalez.com
  Properties for sale by owners

www.mlx.com
  Listings of co-op apartments for sale in New York City

www.robertsrules.com
  Robert's Rules of Order

www.realtorreprints.com
   Reprints of articles published by the National Association
   of Realtors

www.condoflipping.com
   Vehicle for buyers and sellers of condo flips

condos@bellsouth.net
   How to contact the author, Denise Evans

Index

About the Author

Denise L. Evans is the author of *How To Make Money on Foreclosures* and the upcoming *Checklists for First-Time Home Buyers*. She is a regular contributor of real estate and business articles for local newspapers, and a popular seminar speaker on real estate topics. She graduated from the University of Alabama School of Law and is a member of the Texas Bar. Ms. Evans is a licensed real estate broker, and an active member of both the Commercial Real Estate Club of Birmingham and the Birmingham chapter of Commercial Real Estate Women. She is also a research associate for the Alabama Real Estate Research and Education Center and a candidate for the coveted CCIM (Certified Commercial Investment Member) designation.

For over twenty years, Ms. Evans and her husband have bought, sold, and developed a wide variety of real estate investments, some on a shoestring and some with more generous financial resources, but always using the same principles, and always at a handsome profit. She resides with her husband in Tuscaloosa, Alabama.